Beyond the Field Trip

Teaching and Learning in Public Places

by Uma Krishnaswami

LINNET PROFESSIONAL PUBLICATIONS
NORTH HAVEN, CONNECTICUT

KH

First published 2002 as a Linnet Professional Publication,
an imprint of The Shoe String Press, Inc.,
2 Linsley Street, North Haven, Connecticut 06473.
www.shoestringpress.com

Library of Congress Cataloging-in-Publication Data

Krishnaswami, Uma, 1956–
  Beyond the field trip : teaching and learning in public places / by Uma
Krishnaswami.
     p. cm.
  Includes bibliographical references and index.
  ISBN 0–208–02501–4 (trade paperback : alk. paper)
     1. School field trips. 2. Activity programs in education. I. Title.

LB1047 .K73 2001
371.3'84—dc21

2001038496

The paper in this publication meets the minimum requirements
of American National Standard for Information Sciences–
Permanence of Paper for Printed Library Materials,
ANSI Z39.48–1984. ∞

Designed by Dutton & Sherman
Printed in the United States of America

11/22/04

To Deb Neubert

Contents

$\mathcal{A}$CKNOWLEDGMENTS

$\mathcal{I}$ *am grateful to all* those who helped me find the path that led to this book. Judyth Hill first got me thinking about teaching writing in special places. Terry Nichols of Aztec Ruins National Monument, setting extraordinary, gave me space to translate ideas into reality. Many thanks to Ann Bond, Kristie Borchers and the San Juan National Forest Artists-in-Residence Program; to Linda Angst and Lucia Pierce of the Arthur M. Sackler Gallery/Smithsonian Institution; to Sue Borchers and the poets of San Antonio Elementary School, Socorro, New Mexico; to Sherril Moon, for her help with the special needs chapter; to Sally Canzoneri; to my husband Sumant, for helping me find all the questions you can ask about a piece of art in the park; to Sonja Horoshko, for showing me how art and writing can speak the same language; and to Stephanie Harvey, for her inspirational work on teaching and writing. And of course thank you, Frank Allison, Kristine Ashworth, Anita Burgess, Ivon Rhoads, Shannon Waller, Dana Reed, Lynne Spence, Diane Mittler, Ginny Jones, Helen Delahunty, Vickie Whitaker, and all those teachers willing to break down comfortable structure in pursuit of "real" learning. Many people gave generously of their time, expertise, program materials, ideas, and more—among them were David Cowan, Dennis Garvin and Marilyn duFour, Joy Hakim, Kristine O'Connell George, Sidney Williams, Reggie Smith and Joe Johnson, Vince de Forrest, Ken Voorhis, Deb Hart, Jeff Creswell, and Matt Mooney. Most of all, to Tasha Deschenie, Gabrielle MacDonald, Kayla Cline, and all the students I've worked with over the years, who have found miracles in old buildings, paintings, birds' nests, and spots on butterfly wings—thank you all, many times over.

INTRODUCTION

Teaching in Public Places

Consider the following field trip: A fourth grade class is visiting a park and museum about forty miles from school. The children jam into the bus at 8:30 A.M. Notebooks and pencils are securely in their backpacks. Backpacks are securely zipped shut. Most hand-held electronic games have been confiscated for the day by Ms. A, the teacher, although one, in the back of the bus, seems to have escaped her attention. At the park, the children crowd into the Visitor Center, where a ranger speaks to them about the history of the place, and the rules that must be followed on the trails.

Ms. A has selected a trail ahead of time. The party troops down it. A few fact-hounds listen to the ranger's explanations about what they are seeing. No one takes notes. Most students are just happy to be outdoors, away from the classroom, and part of an experience that everyone knows is unlikely to generate homework. A few, however, have already begun the "how-long-is-this-going-to-take-this-is-boring" refrain.

Lunchtime arrives. Notebooks are extricated from backpacks. After lunch a handout is passed out, with questions beginning "What did you learn about. . . ?" and "What did you observe. . . ?" Some children write with speed, others painfully. A museum visit follows, and the day is over.

Asked what they liked about the trip, the fourth graders are enthusiastic about the skunk the school bus narrowly missed on the road. Some mention specific exhibits in the museum. One asks a question about what they have seen. One comments on how long the trail was. From the back, a lone voice forgets itself and cries out, "Yes! I beat the game!"

This example of a field trip is a composite of images that are true—in this case, all too true. Too often, the process of organizing and carrying out a field trip becomes an end in itself. Rules and the consequences of infringing them govern the day. Getting from Point A to Point B is no more than a nose-counting exercise. Worksheets and advance assignments that are meant to teach particular lessons about the site, serve to provide information, which there is no guarantee the children will know how to use, or why. In reality these things can prevent children from experiencing the place in the only ways that will find hooks in memory, those ways that hold meaning for them. Facts about a place, like any other kind of facts, are of use only if there is a context for the following:

- understanding the facts;
- applying them;
- drawing conclusions from the application;
- interpreting those findings for someone else.

In contrast, consider these two alternate scenarios:

In the wood-beamed rooms of an old Maryland inn, a group of men once met to swig ale and plot, while their tethered horses snorted outside. In this little house, with corn-cob checker pieces and pipes scattered about, the Lincoln assassination plot still casts a long shadow. A group of fifth graders is visiting the Surratt House, the first stopping point on the escape route of an actor turned murderer named John Wilkes Booth. The children have been asked to take notes on the sights, sounds, and smells, as well as any tactile and visceral impressions that might grab them. "Don't worry," Mr. B, the teacher, tells them, "about spelling, or making it look pretty. Just write. Draw, if that helps to get you started."

They all write. Not with equal fluency, or even willingness, but they write. Some jot notes about the patterns of the beams, some about the period costumes of the interpretive guides. One child is captivated by the enormous cast-iron pots in the kitchen; another draws details of a firearms display. A simple choice of subject transforms an onerous task into something palatable, even interesting. One child whines, "I can't. I don't know where to start." But when her attention is drawn to the bed capable of accommodating five people sideways on a busy night, she finds a story line in history that grabs her attention. She pulls out her notebook and gets to work.

Later, over lunch, the children discuss the place. Opinions are divided as to whether innkeeper Mary Surratt was innocent or guilty of helping Booth; whether the trial of the conspirators was fair or not. "People disagreed about this even back in 1865," Mr. B points out.

Returning to school the following day, the class will decide to stage the trial of the conspirators. Mr. B will shelve his plans to move on down the historical time line. Instead, the group will linger awhile with the assassination and its impact upon subsequent events in history. They will build an alternative historical time line, as it might have been had Lincoln not been murdered. And the process of questioning, finding some answers, and asking new questions will lead inevitably to discussion of political assassinations in other times and places. Of transfers of power, peaceful and otherwise. Of how societies swing between order and chaos. The children will also write letters to the Surratt House, expressing their opinions of a proposed road construction project that will have an impact on the museum.

Switch now to the high desert of the Southwest. In the cliff palaces of Mesa Verde, Colorado, only a short hike away from the Visitor Center, dust-streaked light pours down into an underground *kiva*. When you have descended the ladder that is the only entry into this circular room, contemporary reality seems worlds away. Imagine a fourth grade group writing field notes at this site—recording the contrast of texture and color in juniper and rock, examining notches left by stone axes on timber, reflecting upon the inky soot left behind by 800-year-old cooking fires.

Instead of going on as many tours at Mesa Verde as they can cram in, the class decides to focus on one site. Mrs. G, the teacher, generates a few questions. But only a few, because the kids quickly explode with their own. When a boy complains, "I'm hot," one of the group counters, "How did they build all this up here? I feel hot just walking up and down these trails."

The students ask the questions. The teacher helps find some answers. As text she uses the trail guide, some prior knowledge, and most important, the rooms hewn out of the cliff face, smoke traces on a rock ceiling, remnants of original woodwork. As in the case of the group that visited the Surratt House, the focus is on story—the story of the people who lived here, and whose fantastic buildings lie scattered all around. That story contains many gaps in it, from the archeological point of view, and those gaps offer room to ask many questions. What might it have felt like to lie here on a ledge on a dark night, hundreds of years ago, and watch the stars appear? What did the constellations look like, to the people who lived back then? What tales do the garbage heaps tell? What is that orange flower, and did it grow here in that far off time? How did nineteenth century ranchers feel when they stumbled around a corner, following stray cattle, only to come upon these astounding cliff palaces?

The important thing here is that the teacher's own learning is transparent, and any instruction is framed by the questions the kids ask. The teacher has read about the site, and is intrigued by it, but she is no expert—she's as bug-eyed as they are, and as full of questions! What better model for the acquisition of knowledge?

This teacher will take back to the classroom the threads of a story. The class will trace the connections that today's Pueblo people make to their wandering ancestors. This will lead to an investigation of migrations, and the reasons that spark them. They will end up studying wars, natural disasters, and adventure as reasons for the wanderings of peoples all over the world. They will write papers, draw maps, sing songs, make up stories, and read them. And all as a result of one field trip. Later, the teacher will write a grant to get a replica archeological dig that her future classes can use at the school.

The difference between the first field trip and these two examples, based on actual reports from teachers, is evident. The first could have taken place anywhere, and the children taking part are passive recipients of information. The other two, in contrast, are student-driven. They emphasize the process of inquiry over the logistics of the visit itself. They yield tangible results, not in formats generated in advance by the teacher (i.e., a fact sheet, or a form to be completed) but during the process of learning, by the students, often in a wide variety of formats and structures. These results are varied in their focus and scope, as determined by the interests of individual students. Neither of these two units of study will yield twenty-five identical pieces of work. They will also be communicated back to a genuine audience, to whom the information is of interest.

Imagine learning or teaching about the Civil War in the grassy fields of Gettysburg, engaging in the sorts of activities Yale University historian Robin Winks (1992) calls public historiography, in the parks that he sees as "branch campuses of the world's largest university." Imagine studying the first wildflowers of spring at Yellowstone Park. Or tracking crustacean life cycles in the Florida Everglades. This is place-based education, and it uses the wealth of knowledge offered by such settings to support and enrich curricula across content areas. At the same time, it instills in students a sense of ownership of these magnificent places.

The possibilities for its use are endless. Indeed, the list of such rich historic, archeological and natural sites under the umbrella of the United States National Park Service seems itself almost endless. The Park Service encompasses 384 areas covering over 83.3 million acres in forty-nine states, the District of Columbia, American Samoa, Guam, Puerto Rico, and the U.S. Virgin Islands. The areas under Park Service jurisdiction include national parks, monuments, battlefields, military parks, historical parks, historic sites, lakeshores, seashores, recreation areas, and scenic rivers and trails. Also included is the very first cluster of national sites, designated in 1790 with the authorization of the District of Columbia: the National Capital Parks, the National Mall, and the White House.

Of course, it is the stories they hold that make the parks, museums, and historic sites so fabulous. Whether those stories occur on the scale of historical or geological time, or the inner time of the cycles of nature, they fascinate because they are the stuff that imaginations grow on. They have beginnings, middles, and ends. They have characters, plots, and settings—and what settings! The stories sometimes repeat themselves, spiralling off into endless possibility. And each is wrapped in webs of the added lore that people have spun, about the place, about those who lived there, about rocks and plants and stars. Story is everywhere in the kinds of public places that America has chosen to set aside as her national parks.

Wishing to make this treasure trove of information more accessible to young people and those who teach them, the National Park Service has launched the Parks as Classrooms initiative (see appendix 1). Park Service personnel work directly with educators in their communities to provide materials and educational experiences that dovetail with existing curriculum requirements. It is an idea both simple and grand. Parks as Classrooms programs and materials include lesson plans, videos, accredited teacher training, traveling trunks of replica artifacts and natural history objects, kits, and resource packets. Each offering of materials arises out of a specific, local partnership between a particular National Parks site and its neighboring school districts. Many of the final products, however, are also meaningful to schools that are not in geographic proximity to the parks producing them.

Traveling trunks, or collections of samples or replicas, can often be obtained on loan, sometimes for a minimal cost. Many parks are actively reaching out to teachers to field-test curriculum materials and enter into education-related partnerships focusing on research, interpretation, and materials development. Information about specific collaborative programs can be obtained by contacting individual parks.

Also under the Park Service umbrella since 1991 is the Teaching with Historic Places program, initiated by the National Park Service's National Register for Historic Places, and funded in part by the

National Trust for Historic Preservation. While Parks as Classrooms emphasizes a broad range of subjects, depending on the theme of an individual park, Teaching with Historic Places uses properties listed in the National Register of Historic Places to foster the study of such sites as evidence from the past. The program has created a range of products and activities to guide teachers through this process. These include ready-to-use lesson plans, multifaceted education kits, and professional development materials and workshops. Like Parks as Classrooms, this program, too, encourages partnerships among educators, historians, preservationists, interpretive staff, museum specialists, archivists, and others.

Naturally, no one can visit all the places on the Park Service map. Nor does every school district or every homeschooling family have immediate physical access to this vast nationally administered reservoir of information and inspiration. For those who do not, examining materials and activities developed in different park contexts is still of value, because the ideas and approaches they contain can often be modified to suit local circumstances. So while your place- based learning project might not occur in a nationally designated site, it can take place in a special site that has significance to your region, your town or city, and your students. Numerous sources of curriculum-related materials and information (national, state, local, university, and foundation) exist or are being developed for exactly this purpose—to link schools and educators with local historic or natural resource settings. Additionally, the wealth of resources and information available to us today can sometimes serve to blur geographical distance and enlarge the concept of community, so that children in California and Virginia, for example, can take part in an arts project celebrating Yellowstone.

Many different programs are described in this book. Some go from abstract to concrete in the way they are designed, beginning with an idea, then finding the right place to support it. Others begin with place, and the educational objectives fall into position as the program is designed. Although some names have been changed and some identities disguised to honor requests for privacy, all activities detailed have actually been tried with real kids in real places. Natural or historic, officially designated or not, in everyone's educational backyard there is some place that holds a story waiting to be shared. This book is about finding ways, and using a range of tools, to understand that story.

CHAPTER ONE

Teaching Across the Curriculum in Authentic Contexts

Education, like every other profession, has developed its own language, shared by those within the field and mostly mystifying to the outsider. Unfortunately, professional jargon sometimes serves to obscure meaning instead of clarifying it. An example of this are student performance standards, now ubiquitous in just about every state. Standards of student performance, grounded in multiple sources of learning, and on tangible outcomes for students, can spark rich and varied educational programs and experiences. Instead, they are often in danger of being reduced to meaningless arrays of assessment rubrics, task lists, traits and outcomes, and quality benchmarks.

This is a loss to us all, especially to children. The idea of performance standards is really quite simple. It is the notion that we ought to be assessing students based on what they know how to do. Can Cara translate a relationship between quantities from a numerical to an algebraic to a graphic representation? Can Brett write a paragraph on a subject of his choice? These are things we want young people to be able to do—not just in the abstract, but in real contexts, to solve real problems.

Traditional systems of education tend generally to assess the child in a zero-sum way: Is Joe intelligent? Can Jennifer carry a tune? The answers are either yes or no, and they are often thought to carry predictive value. Performance-based instruction on the other hand, assesses children not on the basis of what they *are*, but on what they can *do* now. It also assumes that skills are on a continuum and that students will master them sequentially in order to progress towards changing goals. Public places like parks and museums offer space for children to demonstrate such real skills, by studying real material in context and offering their conclusions back to a real audience. That is the purpose of authentic instruction in a real context, something I will refer to as place-based instruction. It can be used effectively to support the standards toward which almost all teachers are now required to teach.

You will find some assumptions recurring in this book: learning should involve inquiry; it can be driven by place to generate its own inquiry; and it should be interdisciplinary. These assumptions underlie what I call place-based and others have called "site-specific" education. Marc Joel Levitt, storyteller and community activist, directs a project that has resulted in the transformation of an entire school into a museum for the research and display of material concerning working culture, immigration, and technology. Levitt applies to education the concepts and ideas framed by urban architect and professor Dolores Hayden (*The Power of Place*, 1995) who urges us to pay attention to cultural landscape—the combination of natural land forms and human interventions (including buildings) that defines a particular place. In education, says Levitt, it also means paying attention to the everyday history and use of a place, and finding a way to integrate curricular needs into the study of that place. Levitt directs the Charles Fortes Magnet Academy Elementary School project. The school was opened by the Providence, Rhode Island school system in 1997, in a building originally constructed as a factory in 1866. The simple question, "I wonder what was made in this building when it was a factory?" led to the idea of creating a museum within the school. The story of the building, and of the community in which it is located, have become the subject of study. All curriculum areas are approached through thematic study of various aspects of the place. With this project, Levitt and the school staff and administration hope to turn all children into curators. They are building a community garden; developing a postcard project; painting murals; setting up an art gallery of urban and factory-oriented art; creating a chorus to sing songs of working class people and immigrants; creating a virtual tour of the building; and researching and conducting oral histories with people who worked in the factory when it was still open.

Not all place-based instruction is as ambitious or as focused as this, of course, but the approaches I suggest in this book have some characteristics in common with the Charles Fortes project. They result in students being actively engaged as learners, framing questions and working toward greater levels of understanding. They connect students in collaborative endeavors with the larger community, as school reform movements all around the country are seeking to do. And they remind us all that in these days of high stakes testing and global competition, it is possible (even perhaps imperative) that we take the time to create exciting, authentic ways to learn—including some that might even be fun!

The field trip is an obvious point to begin developing a place-based instructional focus. Thinking of it in this way—as part of a broader instructional program—helps turn these selected community sites into real world classrooms. Additionally, this way of thinking diverges sharply from the "bell curve" approach, where you take for granted there will be kids who will "get it" and those who won't, and towards a performance approach where "it" is not a singular nugget of information to be "gotten," but multiple sets of knowledge to be built. Here are some suggestions for the creative use of field trips.

1. Remove the field trip from center stage as a free-standing event.
   Make it instead only one part of a longer process, in which the
   same sets of knowledge will be explored from many different
   angles, both in the classroom and in the field. The learning will
   have begun before you visit the site, and it will continue after you

return. The focus is no longer on getting permission slips and counting noses.

2. Visit the site on your own before you take students there. Know the place. Study the terrain. Read the history. Try the science. You would hardly do less in your own classroom. Begin to think of the site as an extension of your classroom. Begin to think of what questions the place will generate for your students.

3. Plan backwards. Figure out what the ultimate product of the study will be. Then work back to find all the activities you will need to use to get there. What you are doing is building bridges between what students know already, and what you anticipate they will know when you have completed the sequence of activities. The place you visit is one ingredient in this process. The visit is not in itself the objective.

4. Present the place, and let students raise the questions. Adults, after all, are driven to find answers to questions that are of burning importance to them. Children sometimes need the process of generating such questions to be modeled for them, but they too will seek answers more consistently when the questions are their own.

5. Allow choice in study. Rather than expect everyone to gain a certain amount of information about many aspects of the experience, allow the surroundings to soak in, then let children focus on what is of interest to them.

6. Whenever possible, you, the teacher, must join in the process of inquiry, modeling its various facets. If the outcome is to be a piece of writing, the teacher writes along with the students. If it is a science investigation, he or she picks a project to work on. Then when the students share their work, the teacher shares as well. When this shared examination of work is repeated over time it also demonstrates that a task worth doing is also worth revisiting and rethinking.

7. Expect and work toward a product—something tangible, something *real*, whatever the medium selected. Examples are a piece of writing, a set of questions, a story line, an exhibit, a letter, an experiment. These should be generated by the children and shaped by them to reflect their own interests and express their own voices.

8. Present the findings or product to an audience—parents, other classes, the local library, the school board, the county government, the Park Service. That, after all, is what people in the "real world" do. Most meaningful creative projects are generated with potential audiences in mind. Even those that are purely investigative in nature, following a question without regard to application of the findings, are usually shared at some point with both general and specialized audiences.

There are three ways to go about organizing projects like this, if you wish to extend your classroom to a park or museum or historic site or other place that is meaningful in your community:

Using the Resources of the Site

This is the simplest way to enhance your teaching. Call the local planetarium for a list of programs. Get on the museum's mailing list. Find out if the park nearby has an outreach program for teachers. See if any of the sites you're considering has a traveling educational kit, or even a traveling presenter. Perhaps the museum offers teacher in-service programs, so you can acquire behind-the-scenes knowledge. An hour's worth of phone calls can yield a wealth of information, and open up all kinds of possibilities. All of this preliminary material can be used to put together a sequence of activities prior to the actual visit, so that students will be prepared to receive and use the further riches the site itself has to offer.

The kinds of resources and materials public places hold for teachers run a very wide gamut. The National Park Foundation, for example, offers grants to local park units to develop curriculum materials, collaborate with teachers, and even offer direct programming to students. Many state park facilities have developed educational materials that they make accessible to teachers and homeschooling parents.

Some private nonprofit organizations offer a range of residential and daytime field programs for students and adults, in which they provide content and instructional expertise in a particular area. These groups generally operate under an agreement with a federal land partner (National Forest Service, National Park Service, or Bureau of Land Management). Each provides learning opportunities, sometimes for a fee, in a non-advocacy environment. Appendix 5 lists a sample of private nonprofit groups that offer educational programs in public places. The offerings from these and similar organizations range from formal school-year and summer institutes for students and teachers, to teacher in-service training, resource materials, and content-specific curricular support.

Parks and museums can often provide curriculum-related materials in connection with special exhibits or events. The Palm Springs Desert Museum, for instance, offered a comprehensive teacher packet related to a traveling exhibit hosted by the museum, *Recycled Re-Seen: Folk Art from the Global Scrap Heap*. The packet included a vocabulary list, a selection of photographs of objects from the exhibit, information about each object selected, and samplers of student activities and curriculum links (see appendix 2). Note that this museum-developed packet focuses on California standards. Most museum education staff are cognizant of their state educational performance standards and either have or are developing materials to meet those standards.

COLLABORATE WITH INTERPRETATION STAFF AT THE SITE

Interpretation is an overwhelming part of the mission of the kinds of public places considered in this book. Freeman Tilden, in 1957, defined interpretation as "an educational activity which aims to reveal meanings and relationships through the use of original objects, by firsthand experience, and by illustrative media, rather than simply to communicate factual information." Museum docents offer interpretation. Park and forest rangers offer interpretation. For the most part they are eager to collaborate with teachers or other leaders of youth groups. Find out who your interpretive staff are in the places you are considering visiting. Then ask how they can help you develop curriculum ideas and materials that will involve their site.

In order to collaborate effectively with site staff, you must learn to understand the language of curatorial and interpretive staff. This is especially important at a time when historic and natural sites are actually in the position of reaching out to schools and teachers, and beginning to learn the language of curriculum and instruction. You will be far ahead of most in this process if you can understand the goals and objectives of the site you will teach in and their relationship to the community. One good way to understand this perspective is to approach a decision maker on-site (staff titles will vary depending on the size and location of the site) not just with a list of your needs but with an interest in an open-ended discussion of possible collaborations. As many of the programs detailed in this book demonstrate, this is precisely the kind of conversation that has led to dynamic, effective programs enriching the lives of the people they touch.

OFFER YOUR EXPERTISE TO THE SITE

You know some things the on-site folks don't. You know your students. You know what's developmentally appropriate for a given age-range of students. You know the standards and benchmarks for your state, the ones you are expected to teach toward.

You can help interpretive staff in a myriad ways. You can offer feedback on their materials as they are developing them. You can field-test any curriculum materials they might be working on and trying to pilot. You might even be able to help them write grants to fund a program that will involve your students. Interpretive staff and teachers working together can make a formidable team! And it is far more rewarding being a partner in a program than merely a consumer of services.

Successful collaborative projects involving public places and local school systems are extremely diverse in nature. Each is crafted to meet the needs of local teachers and students, and to use local talent in implementation. Each results in forging links between groups and people, people and place.

Sam H. Ham, in his book, *Environmental Interpretation* (1992) suggests one way to arouse interest in parks and historic places is to capitalize on traditional celebrations in an area. Almost every town has some kind of historical or cultural celebration linked to place. The "Return of the Salmon" festival is an example, held annually in Leavenworth, Washington. There are festivals throughout the country dedicated to music, chili, dance, art, history, peace, justice, and even garlic! Maple festivals abound in northeastern regions of the United States and many parts of Canada. Fiesta days and Heritage days are other examples of local events offering a combination of education and entertainment to the general public. While Ham's suggestions for creating local happenings are aimed at interpretive staff in public places, such celebrations provide many opportunities (poster contests, music and drama performances, and booths with local goods for sale are a few examples) for local schools to become involved as more than observers of the event.

In Arizona's Glen Canyon National Recreation Area, high school advanced biology students conduct "real" science in a national park setting as part of their coursework. Students have worked on growing endangered razorback suckers in ponds on the Lake Powell Golf Course, for release into the San Juan River inflow tributaries. They have also carried out wintertime testing of Lake Powell water for the presence of *E.coli*, or fecal coliform, bacteria.

In all these instances the point of departure from "the field trip" was the seeking out of essential questions to study. What was the forest like before we began managing fire? What is the bacterial presence in lake water during months when the administering agency does not carry out water testing? In California, in the Santa Monica Mountains National Recreation Area, children get to try on costumes of the *Ranchero* period and process, through a sequence of activities, what it must have been like to live at that time in that place. Through a different set of experiences, they learn about the legacy of the Shumash people and the meaning of this place to them. They drill holes in abalone shells using replica tools. They ask questions about the use of the land, and its significance to all the people who have ever passed through there.

In Missouri, the Arch of St. Louis is the setting of exciting educational activities. Developed in collaboration with local educators, outreach programs include both trips to the museum and visits to schools by park interpreters. At the museum, children engage in learning about the overland trail experience of pioneers heading West through journaling and dramatic presentations of their travel. The resources of the parks can enhance education both in the classrooms and on-site.

In each of these examples, children worked on a product, whether that was a data set or a piece of art or a journal. This raises the issue of how these outcomes are to be evaluated. Assessing performance of real tasks is considerably more complicated than grading a test. Many elementary school teachers use a TOW assessment model: Terrific/OK/ Needs Work. This is an easy way for both student and teacher to judge tasks. The teacher, in consultation with the students, decides on a list of tasks that will be accomplished during a given project. Then after the tasks are done, each is referenced to that original list, and can be assessed by both students and teacher on this three-point scale.

But TOW is still an external evaluation system, reflective of the teacher's judgment. The very use of terms such as "Terrific" or "OK" is subjective. How does one rate art, for example, on such a scale? There is no way it can be used by adults to critique each other's work, to promote higher quality and greater professionalism. For that, the scale has to be geared toward establishing greater and greater self-evaluation.

A more natural way of looking at the tasks developed in a place-based learning activity is to use what my students sometimes call the "punctuation scale." It uses symbols instead of words, and they are referenced, not to an abstract rating of the good or poor quality of work, but to what has been achieved, and what remains to be accomplished.

"PUNCTUATION SCALE" FOR SELF- AND TEACHER EVALUATION

Symbol	*Meaning*
+	What works in this product (story, poem, model, experimental setup)?
?	What raises questions?
*	What needs to be fixed, now or when the project is shared with an audience?

This is so simple a format it seems obvious. It translates easily to assessment by self, other, and teacher. Many teachers prefer not to grade work that emerges from so rich an experience as place-based learning. If you must grade, however, using this format can initiate a process directly comparable to the critical reflection that adult professionals use when reviewing their own work or that of others in real processes of inquiry.

Chapter Two

Writing in Special Places

Parks, museums, nature trails, forests all have story in common. Sometimes that story lies in historical narrative; sometimes within the cycles of nature; at other times behind a particular exhibit, or type of art or artifact. Writing, of course, offers the perfect set of tools for finding, uncovering, and relating story. So using the tools and processes of writing is a natural way to help young people access and process the story behind these special places.

When I first moved to northwestern New Mexico I had the good fortune to cross paths with Judyth Hill, a poet who has spent the last twenty years working with young people through writing in parks, museums, and on natural and historic trails. Judyth holds that just as adult writers write out of their real life experiences, out of their response to place and story, so too must children. (See appendix 3 for samples from the poetry curriculum she developed for the Georgia O'Keeffe Museum in Santa Fe.) "When you work with children," she says, "you have to affirm that their experience has value. Exposing children to beautiful, powerful places and to writing gives them a way to make these connections."

As a result of my conversations with Judyth, the Aztec Ruins

Children's Writing Project was born and nurtured. This is a week-long fiction writing workshop in an eight hundred-year-old ancestral Pueblo (so-called "Anasazi") setting. It is offered to school groups from third through fifth grade, takes place on the trail and back in the classroom, and culminates in a Young Authors' Reading open to the public.

Aztec Ruins National Monument is a National Park Service site, part of an incredible network of prehistoric communities linked by pottery and architectural styles, and by astounding webs of strategically placed roads. Like many other ancestral Pueblo sites, it is considered to have been constructed in the twelfth century A.D. People in New Mexico's Pueblo communities trace ancestral linkages back to the people who built these pre-Columbian cities. Aztec Ruins has been designated a World Heritage Site, and over sixty thousand tourists visit it annually. Yet as of 1997, only a handful of area teachers had ever brought their students there, and then only for the obligatory field trip in connection with a Southwest studies unit. Once, when I visited a school only eleven miles from the monument, a fourth grader informed me in all earnestness that the ruins were built by ancient Aztecs! This child was no better informed than the early English settlers responsible for the misnomer. For the most part, the rich array of archeological and cultural resources available at the monument were being left untapped.

But the Park Service personnel at Aztec Ruins were beginning to reach out to teachers. Through a Parks as Classrooms grant (see appendix 1), they were developing lesson plans, grounding them in the then-newly issued New Mexico State Educational Standards and Benchmarks, and field-testing them with groups of students and teachers. They had also created replica artifacts chests that were available on loan to schools. It was a perfect time to launch a writing program.

Luckily for me, Theresa Nichols, chief of interpretation at the monument, thought so too. We began with one pilot third grade class in fall 1997, and have since then been able to offer four workshops a year. Since then, the project has been funded by grants from New Mexico Arts (a division of the State Office of Cultural Affairs), the National

Endowment for the Arts, Burlington Resources Foundation, and the National Park Foundation. The sessions fill up almost as soon as they are announced, and a workshop is planned for area teachers on teaching in public places such as Aztec Ruins.

The project consists of the following activities:

1. Soon after the start of the school year in the fall, teachers sign their classes up for the workshop. Classes are selected based on this application. See sample Teacher Application Form on pages 14–15.

2. Six weeks prior to the workshop, a planning session is held that includes the participating teacher; parents who will take part in the field trip or help on the day of the Young Authors' Reading; aides if any; and the writer-in-residence (in this instance, me).

PLANNING MEETING

Roles of participants

- Students: writers
- Parents: help with any special needs; guide small groups; help with refreshments and setup at Young Authors' Reading
- Teacher: facilitator; oversee stories/illustrations; direct rehearsal for reading
- Writer-in-residence: facilitator; oversee stories; produce stories for display
- Parks staff: write and send out press releases; take pictures; photocopy and help with materials; assist with reading
- Local businesses: donate refreshments for reading

Guidelines for workshop

- Writing will be fiction, and all content will be original. There is no stipulation as to length of story.
- General introduction to fiction writing will be provided on the day of the workshop.

TEACHER APPLICATION FORM

Aztec Ruins Children's Writing Project

Name of teacher:_____

Name and address of school:_____

Phone # of school:_____

Grade of students:_____

Any information pertinent to your students:_____

_____

_____

Preferred schedule: Pick a month and we will consult you to determine actual date.

☐ November 2001   ☐ December 2001

☐ February 2002   ☐ March 2002

Please write a few sentences here on what you hope your students will gain from this workshop:

_____

_____

Also please note that in order for your students to be involved in this program, we will require the following commitments from your school:

1. Bus transportation for students. Two round trips from school to Aztec Ruins: the first to tour the monument and begin writing stories there; the second for the Young Authors' Reading.
2. Bag lunches for those students who have free or reduced-price lunches. We ask that students bring a bag lunch for the first session, which runs from about 9:00 A.M. to 1:30 P.M.

3. In-kind contributions in the form of the following materials: time at computer/printer for final printing of stories; computer diskettes; markers; colored construction paper for display of completed work; materials needed to prepare art-work for display.

4. Art materials for students to use in illustrating stories. We will work with you to determine medium to be used for illustration. Stories will be displayed at Aztec Ruins Visitor Center; selected stories may be submitted for publication.

5. The commitment of time to this project, as follows:
   - 1 day at Aztec Ruins with resident writer/artist, and traditional Pueblo presenter, for field trip/tour and writing workshop;
   - 1-2 days in school to complete, revise, and illustrate stories;
   - 1-2 days in school with resident writer to edit and prepare manuscripts for display;
   - 1/2 day at Aztec Ruins for Young Authors' Reading.

6. Two or three parent volunteers to assist with one-to-one or small group needs on field trip, and with day-of-event work at the Young Authors' Reading.

We also ask that you commit to the philosophy and intent of this program, which is to give students the tools, setting, and the emotional/creative space to write. No content is disallowed, but the rules of fiction writing are made known and expected to be followed. Please make sure that you discuss the content and teaching approaches used in this program with the resident writer, so that we can make the program fit in as seamlessly as possible with your curriculum.

As collaborating teacher, you will be responsible for obtaining the necessary releases from families for field trips, photographs, publication of stories, display of stories at Aztec Ruins, radio readings of stories, newspaper articles, or other publicity preceding or following the Young Authors' Reading.

- Drafts will focus on content more than neatness, spelling, grammatical correctness.
- Spelling and grammar will be addressed during editing/revision phase.
- All children will be expected to write one completed story of their own creation.
- The site must be part of the story in any way the children choose. All children will share their stories at a public reading.

Guidelines for behavior management on field trip

- Children will generate the rules for appropriate behavior on the trail, including rules particular to that site, and will be held to these rules.
- Only positive reinforcement will be used.

Special needs

Any children with special needs will be identified at this stage, and reasonable accommodations/assistance determined.

Logistics

Dates, times, and other details are also decided at this meeting.

3. One to three days before the first field trip, the writer-in-residence meets with students. This first workshop session, which usually lasts about half a day, covers a number of questions related to both fiction writing and the setting to be explored.

WORKSHOP SESSION HELD IN SCHOOL BEFORE FIRST FIELD TRIP

Aztec Ruins: What is this place? What's special about it? Why should we care?

What is fiction? How is it different from other kinds of writing? Some reflections on truth and lies and where they intersect in good fiction.

Fiction gives permission to the writer to tell lies, but there is truth at the heart of all powerful stories. If you're going to tell lies, be sure to tell really good ones, even grand ones! Hold to the rules of the kind of story you are telling. E.g., if it's historical fiction, get the history part right. If it's science fiction, make sure the science is plausible or at least builds on what we know today. Stories must have their own logic.

What are the ingredients of a story? Character=Who? Plot=What? Setting=Where? When? Under what circumstances?

Activities on the field trip: Roles and expectations of all participants, children and adults for the workshop. Every writer will write one completed story of his/her own creation. The ruins must be part of the story in any way the writer chooses. All writers will share their stories at a public reading.

Logistics: What to bring; what not to bring; what to wear.

4. First field visit. On this day, four very important things happen:

- The children tour the site, ask questions, and the place begins to work its magic.
- We start to jot down notes on the things that fascinate us.
- We meet with a traditional presenter from one of the New Mexico pueblos whose people trace migratory and spiritual links to Aztec Ruins. This is of particular importance to this project, given the many prevailing stereotypes of Native American peoples, and the lack of widespread access to information from the Native perspective.
- In the reconstructed Great Kiva, likely to have been a spiritual and ceremonial center in this place, the children begin the process of turning initial notes into the beginnings of stories.

**TEACHER/FACILITATOR INTERVENTIONS, EARLY STAGES OF
SHAPING NOTES INTO STORIES**

Teacher interventions are best shaped into questions at this stage.
Use them strategically with writers who seem stalled, unable to
make the leap from descriptive note-taking to imaginative story
writing. Here are some sample questions.

- Do you know yet who's in your story? Animal? Girl? Boy?
  Alien?
- Who is your main character? Who should the reader care
  about?
- Does your story happen now, or long ago? How long ago?
  Or in the future?
- Does your story happen all at one point in time? Or does
  your character travel through time?
- What did you think was interesting or strange or funny on
  the tour? What might happen if you just begin your story
  at that point?
- What might happen if you took your main character to
  that place, or point, and started things happening?
- Have you told a grand lie yet? Is it time to do that in your
  story?
- What does your character want? Dream of? Hope for?
  What must he/she overcome to get that wish or realize that
  dream?
- Do you know how she/he will go about that getting/realiz-
  ing?
- Is there a villain in your story? Does there need to be?
- Whose point of view are you telling this story from?
- Close your eyes and see your character. What is he/she
  doing?
- Listen to your character speak. What is she/he saying?

Bennie Romero and students at Aztec Ruins. *Courtesy of Aztec Ruins National Monument*

An important part of the first field visit is the building of two distinct vocabularies. The first is the vocabulary of the place itself. At Aztec Ruins, that includes the following words:

ANCESTORS

ANCESTRAL PUEBLO—a recently adopted term to refer to people who once lived throughout the Colorado Plateau and Southwest, and who are ancestors of many Southwestern American Indians today.

ARCHEOLOGY—the study of past human cultures and the material evidence they leave behind.

ARTIFACT—any object made or used by humans.

DESCENDANTS

KIVA—room with distinctive features, usually underground, for ceremonial use.

LATILLA—cottonwood or aspen pole placed in a roof.

MIDDEN—an area where discarded items were deposited.

VIGA—a log of spruce, fir, ponderosa pine, or juniper, used as the support beam in a roof.

Our vocabulary of place also includes possible names, provided by our Pueblo cultural presenters, for characters in stories—because of course if you happen to be writing a story set in pre-Columbian times, you cannot name your characters Bill and Sarah!

Bear in mind that each place you choose to visit and study, whether it is a historic site, a museum, or a park, will have its own vocabulary. Part of studying a place is learning to use its language and that of the professionals who care for it.

The other vocabulary we build is that of story. As we write together, we learn words such as character, plot, setting, and dialogue. We also come across concepts such as point of view, voice, and psychic distance. These are complex constructs, but it is possible to find a range of examples of each in the stories students write. When they are explained in context, it is amazing how children who are quite young can understand and use them. Through the day, as the stories start to form, we get together in small groups as needed to discuss these writing topics.

5. The afternoon of the first field visit day is spent at the Visitor Center, where the children continue working on their stories. As the teacher and I circulate, reading work in progress, parents and other accompanying adults take small groups into the museum area to look at artifacts, or back on the trail to see or touch or smell again the things that are beginning to work their way into the stories.

At the end of this first day, everyone is exhausted. And short or long, scribbled or tidy, the children (and most of the adults) leave with at least the beginning of a story.

6. Back at school, I spend blocks of time over the next week working on the stories with the children. We revise, rewrite, and edit. The teacher and I read each child's story, and consult on ways to move the process forward, to help each child write the best and brightest prose he or she can possibly produce. We use a process of developmental editing— teasing out the components of the story, adding and deleting and shifting text. During the week, I work with parents to type finalized stories into the computer. No changes are made without consulting with the writer. Together we serve not ourselves, but the story. Somewhere along the way, I also manage to write a piece myself, and consult with teacher and parents on the children's writing.

STORY DEVELOPMENT AND EDITING PROCESS

Each of these can be a point of discussion.

Story development

Is there enough happening in the story? Is the writer rushing to finish? Is there a logical progression to the story? If this is historical fiction, is the "history" part accurate? If this is fantasy (e.g., time travel) is there a return? Or if not, is there a twist, offering a surprise ending? Do we care enough about the main character? Does the character grow or change by the story's end? Does the setting come through vividly? Is the plot consistent? Is the beginning at the right point, or is there pre-writing that might need to be edited out?

Style

Does the story flow smoothly? Do the words sing? Do they carry an authentic voice? Are the best possible words chosen? Can clichéd words or phrases be replaced by stronger and more original ones? Are character names well chosen? Is point of view clear? Is the ending satisfying?

Copyediting

Do spelling and grammar conform with standard usage? Do they depart from it only when they need to, for example, in dialogue? Are tense and person consistent? Are there paragraphs? Are they indented? Is dialogue punctuated appropriately? Are exclamation marks used effectively and not extravagantly?

The question invariably arises of whether it is acceptable to have violence in a story. My position on this is that violence is part of life, and therefore it can be part of story. Violence is acceptable in a story if the story needs it, and if it is part of a larger chain of events. The writer must offer a plausible explanation of motivation. Large numbers of people must not be killed off for no reason. Just as endless sweetness is boring, so is excess of blood. Also, if the story is told in the first person, the writer may not kill off the main character or who will tell the rest of the story? (I did have one writer get around this by having the main character die, and then come back as a ghost!)

7. While revisions are simmering all around, the children are also working on interpreting the place in visual art. Here we have had a huge range of materials and processes used, including pen and ink, watercolor, pastels, crayon-resist work, and collage. Most recently, Colorado artist Sonja Horoshko and I led a session together, writing and creating art at the same time. Each child ended with a story and a large piece of art, drawn with hand-made willow charcoal on 2' x 2' squares of masonite that had first been covered with white gesso, then finished in acrylic paints. The images were glowing and beautiful. An example is Peter Hornbecker's piece, *Untitled*, showing the rows of doorways that are a feature of the rooms at Aztec Ruins.

When Sonja and I led the workshop together, this part of the process really came to life. We threw the desks out into the hallway, spread black plastic bags on the floor, and painted and wrote in the same room. Magical things began to happen. The words and images flowed in and out of each other. Art took on narrative quality. Stories incorporated themes from the images. Some children drew from the stories of others, or wrote to the paintings of others. Watching Sonja

Untitled by Peter Hornbecker, fourth grade, Ladera del Norte Elementary School, Farmington, NM (2001, acrylic on masonite). *Courtesy of Aztec Ruins National Monument*

working with the children, swapping palettes, mixing colors, I began to understand that the language of art and writing are not that different.

8. As the week nears its end, we approach the grand finale, the Young Authors' Reading. To get ready for this, the children practice reading the stories out loud, the teacher practices his or her introduction, and I practice mine. We all critique each other on phrasing and vocal range, posture, and all the other stage presence issues that writers who read their work out loud often secretly worry about.

9. Finally, we celebrate the entire hectic, wonderful, intense week at the Young Authors' Reading. Families come to hear and see. The stories, typed and illustrated, are on display in the museum area of the Visitor

Center. A newspaper or television reporter might drop by. An instructor from the teacher training program at the local college occasionally brings her students. And under a spotlight, against a case of black-on-white pottery, "Mesa Verdean period," the teacher and I do our introductory bits and fade away, and the children read their work. Some read loudly and proudly, others timidly. Yet others ham for parental cameras. But they all read stories, and the stories are theirs. Here is one.

THE GIRL AND THE MAGICAL GRINDING STONE

by Gabrielle McDonald

There once lived a girl, with her mother, father, and two sisters. The two sisters were mean to the girl. They picked on her. They made her work. They laughed at her. Sometimes they made her cry.

One morning, the girl wandered off, and she found a strange grinding stone. It glowed in different colors. It felt very warm when she picked it up. She brought it home to show her parents.

When she brought it home, everyone was amazed. But then her sisters kept on bothering her. "Give it to us!" they said.

The girl picked up the stone and wished her sisters would leave her alone. Then pouf! Her sisters disappeared.

The girl was happy that her two sisters were gone.

The girl got hungry. She wished that she had some corn bread and turkey stew. Pouf! A warm pot of stew came from nowhere. A delicious crumbly handful of piki bread appeared, just for her. She ate it all, and was happy.

Next, her mother came along and asked her to go gather some firewood.

But the girl said, "I wish you would go away."

And pouf! Her mother disappeared.

Now she was frightened that her mother was gone forever.

She made a last wish. "Please make everything come back to normal," she wished.

And it did. The mean sisters came back too—but they were nicer to her.

The girl went out again and she buried the magical grinding stone. If you visit Aztec Ruins, and you go to the wall with a green stripe, you will see a big stand of dried grass. That is where the magical grinding stone is buried.

I chose fiction as the genre in the setting of Aztec Ruins for two reasons. First, I was intrigued by the many possibilities it offered children to wonder about a place still surrounded by many archeological questions. Second, fiction writing has its own internal logic that imposes demands on the writer.

This is not to say that other genres of writing cannot be employed successfully when writing in special places. But the form you choose must work for the place you are in, and that is a decision that can be made with a little advance planning and foresight. If you are thinking of turning an upcoming field trip into a writing experience, consider the following:

- How large or small an area will you cover on the trail or museum walk?
- How much prerequisite learning will students require in order to successfully produce the outcome you are targeting? This will vary with the complexity of the material, and whether questions raised by the content will promote or overwhelm interest.
- How many stops have you planned for note taking? Where are the stops?
- How long will you be at the site? Three hours? All day? Overnight?
- Is this a one-time trip, or will you come back?
- Is there a space you can adjourn to that can serve as a classroom? A room is good, but not essential. Under a tree or in the shadow of a building or cliff can work too. But there needs to be

Coyote's Cloud by Tasha Deschenie, third grade, Country Club Elementary School, Farmington, NM (2000, pencil). *Courtesy of Aztec Ruins National Monument*

some designated place where the children can review their notes and begin to transform them into first drafts.

• Where and how will the final sharing of finished work take place? Back in school or on-site?

There are two other considerations to bear in mind: first, what kind of writing outcomes seem most logical, given the rest of your writing curriculum? And second, is there a particular product (e.g., field observations, poetry, a trail guide) that the site itself needs and might be most willing to display or publish?

Length of time available for the writing project might seem another consideration at the outset, but time does not necessarily help define selection of genre. It might appear that poetry needs less time than, say, a story, or a trail guide. But anyone who has spent weeks struggling with the choice of just the right word, or juggling words in the wait for the perfect phrase to shape itself, knows that the length of a written piece is not always in direct proportion to the time spent working on it! Shorter is often longer.

I have taught versions of this place-based writing workshop at the Smithsonian Institution's Arthur M. Sackler Gallery, a museum of Asian art in Washington, D.C., and in San Juan National Forest in southwestern Colorado. In each of these places, there is something about the place itself, about real works of art or antiquity, or the immediacy of rivers, forests, and bird song, that breaks through the boundaries between content areas and sets the imagination wandering. When you are writing a poem or a story or an article, it does not matter whether the source of your information is history or geology. And so cross-curricular instruction, something teachers have long labored over, becomes real and tangible and natural, even to the reluctant writers in a group.

EXAMPLES OF WRITING ACTIVITIES THAT INVOLVE ACTIVE AND AUTHENTIC LEARNING

Gathering information

- Examine selected pieces of art or objects, and note your observations.
- Observe trees on a trail, and jot down as many observations as you can in 5 minutes.
- Sketch for 5 minutes, then write about what you sketched.
- Examine the walls of a historic building, and write down what you notice.

Generating questions

- What questions are left unanswered by your observations?
- Can you identify everything you observed?
- What questions might you ask the people who lived here? The people who made this art? The people who built this building?

Synthesizing knowledge

- Think about what an object or piece of art reminds you of. If it's old, what else might have been going on in the world when it was created?
- If you were the artist/builder, what tools would you have to work with?
- How would this place have looked 100 years ago?

Drawing conclusions

- See if you can pull two things into your story that you didn't know before you came here.
- Take an unusual point of view in telling a story or writing a poem. Be the artist or builder, or a chip of paint or mortar, or a mouse in the woodpile, watching. See how looking through different eyes changes a piece of writing.

Presenting a meaningful product

- Revise, revise, revise!
- Get your work ready for display.
- Get your work ready to be read.
- Make sure your work gets back to the site you visited in some form.

Those who teach writing must themselves write. I decided long ago never to assign a writing task I had not tried myself. I believe this is critically important for teachers of writing. If you don't know what it's like to stare at a blank page and feel your ideas fall to dust around you, how can you help children get beyond that stage? Teachers who write themselves, and gain the courage to share unfinished work with their students, are modeling the writing process for those students far more effectively than any number of advance organizers and writing formats possibly can. In the Aztec Ruins Children's Writing Project we all write—teachers, parents, and I. And so of course the children write too. Not a child has yet emerged from the workshops without a story.

The other important fact that drives this process is that the stories will, without exception, be edited, finalized, and then displayed for families, friends, and total strangers to read. Tourists from all over the world will get to read them. It is exactly the sobering thought of the audience to come, after all, that keeps writers in the real world focused despite the tedium of revision.

And then there is the question of whether it takes a writer to teach writing. Undoubtedly, a writer who has experienced both the joys and frustrations of the writing life can bring this alive for children in a way that no one else can, in the same way that physicists or geographers passionate about their work can set young imaginations on fire. Judyth Hill suggests that teachers who want to bring their writing classes to life get in touch with their local or regional or state arts councils, and find local writers to join and enrich their students' classroom and field trip experiences. (See appendix 4 for a list of state arts councils.) Teachers should also begin to nurture their own writing skills.

Although not all writers teach, an increasing number are finding their way into classrooms. Teachers and Writers is a New York-based group that English professor and writer Peter Elbow calls "a community of people committed to teaching and writing and to the idea that these two activities belong together" (see appendix 1). Writers are also beginning to make their presence felt in museums, parks, and historic sites, to run or assist with some form of writing activity with young people. In Houston, Texas, Writers in the Schools runs a program in which students visit the Menil Collection, a Houston gallery. They write in response to the contemporary art they see there. They work with a resident writer, both in the gallery and back in school, and then read their work. Judyth Hill began her Poetry-in-Place workshops at the Museum of the Horse in Ruidoso, New Mexico.

And finally, a word on allowing students to choose what they write about. Writing is richest and strongest when the writer deals with subjects that are personally stirring, exciting, or thought-provoking. So in a writing workshop in the context of a special place, the only content rule should be that the place must somehow be incorporated into the narrative. It can serve as setting, or lend texture. More directly, the place itself or some component or feature of it can be the subject of the writing. Other than that, young writers must be allowed to find their own voices by asking the questions that interest them. The obvious advantage to this is that in historic places, museums, and natural settings, such questions are all around. The alternative, the teacher-assigned topic, will result in twenty-odd identical pieces of work. We surely have enough of those!

Chapter Three

Ways to Understand the Past

It is easy to think of history as a series of events, sequential, neatly docketed, dated, and filed. But think of this example of history as it occurs within families—the kind of history every child and adult knows intimately:

Step 1. Ask someone in your family (your mother, aunt, older sister) about something that happened when she was younger (ten or twenty years ago). Tell her to describe the event in her own words. Write it down.

Step 2. Now ask someone else in your family (father, uncle, cousin) about the same event. Tell him to describe it in his own words. Write it down.

Step 3. Now ask yet another relative (an aunt, an uncle, a grandparent).

Now that you have all this documentation of an event that everyone agrees occurred, think about the following two questions:

1. How many versions of this piece of family history will you get?

2. Which one is true?

The truth is, history is much more than a series of dates, beginning at a defined time and ending in the present. The past has many renderings, not all of which even include the same sets of occurrences. History is actually more like a giant tapestry, with many threads contributing to the design, and with different groups of people shining the light of public acceptance on one part of the picture or the other. It all happened, true. But it's seen differently by different people because they have their own individual perspectives. Points of view might also differ among people from different generations, and those from different ethnic, socioeconomic, cultural, and religious groups. People who were close to the events concerned will feel passionately about these differences. History, quite simply, is what happens when "now" becomes "then." Public places such as parks and museums offer a wealth of resources for understanding that process of transformation.

Writer Joy Hakim, known for *A History of Us,* her series of books that bring American history to life for children, says of her own research process, "I read, read, read. Everything I can find. I also visit places I'm writing about if I can. Sometimes I call experts in the field." Hakim says the story in history is what captivates, and urges teachers to use multiple resources of people and print and place to help students grasp its essence.

One way to learn about various periods of history is through reading well-written fiction and nonfiction. But be aware that children, especially in the early grades, do not know the difference between historical fiction and history. As Joy Hakim puts it, "Good historical fiction is wonderful, if labeled and understood as fiction. Help students know the facts from the fiction." In her own work, Hakim also makes sure her writing is read (before publication) by those she respects— that means historians, educators, friends, and now that she is writing science books, physicists. She actually pays children to read and edit her work. "Editors get paid," she says, "why shouldn't kids?"

Hakim's is a process capable of replication in the classroom, in connection with a visit to a historical site:

1. Read everything you can find about a place or its story before you visit it.

2. Write about the place when you're there.

3. Revise your work when you return.

4. Read each others' work.

5. Send your writing back to the place you visited, either by presenting it at a reading, or arranging for it to be exhibited.

Margot Fortunato Galt, in her book *The Story in History: Writing Your Way into the American Experience* (1992), offers a very simple, very sound reason for teaching history and writing simultaneously. She suggests that using creative writing as a means of accessing history is likely to spark the imaginations of those students who will otherwise slip through American history classes having grabbed at only a few random facts. Creative writing is about infusing the writer's ideas, the writer's imagination, into the process of understanding—precisely what teachers of history would like to have happen among their students. Galt uses her own "Ode to the Peanut" as an example of research presented through the medium of poetry. It is chock-full of facts—distilled, personalized, and rendered as delectable and consumable as peanut brittle, as these lines show:

> 300 miracle recipes
> of George Washington
> Carver
> to turn
> the boll weevil
> South to gold.

It is this consuming of the facts and then reshaping them in a personal way that most of us have never experienced. Most history taught in school is presented second-hand. Someone else has done the research, and what is taught and learned are the canned facts. An exciting way to make history come alive is to use primary sources—the sources that historians use to understand the past. These are available to all of us, in the form of newspaper archives, census records, passenger arrival lists for major ports, court proceedings, birth and death records, military records, land records, maps, diaries—the list could go on. Each historic site you visit has its own treasure trove of primary sources. Additional relevant material can be found in local libraries, historical societies, churches, and city or county records offices. Studying samples of primary sources of information about a place or about the content of a museum exhibit, before your field trip, can be a wonderful warm-up activity. Studying these sources after the visit can be a way to reinforce knowledge acquired first-hand.

What both primary sources and historic objects and places offer is the chance to forge a tangible, experiential connection with the past. In Montgomery County, Maryland, Reginald Smith and Stephen Durand have taken this idea to its ultimate extension. The Muncaster Challenge Program is an alternative school for middle school students considered both troubled and troubling by the school system, referred for expulsion by their principals. One of the programs at Muncaster uses the stories and places of history to help these students find their own place in today's world. Each year since 1998, students and educators recreate the past for themselves by re-enacting it. In the first Muncaster experience, students followed part of the trail taken by teenaged Ann Maria Weems, who fled from enslavement in 1855, traveling from Rockville, Maryland, to Canada. Since that first journey, students have biked, hiked, or boated down significant stretches of the paths taken by people escaping slavery in the days of the Underground Railroad. They have met families who number escaped enslaved Americans among their ancestors.

The International Network to Freedom Association (INTFA) is a grassroots collaborative promoting racial harmony, and education about the Underground Railroad. The Park Service and INTFA together helped plan and pay for the Muncaster students to undertake Journey to Freedom II, a re-enactment of "the *Pearl* affair," in which seventy-seven people escaped from slavery in Alexandria, Georgetown, and Washington City (as the nation's capital was called then), in April 1848. Among the people aboard the schooner *Pearl* were six children of Paul and Amelia Edmonson from the Norbeck area of Montgomery County. Students retracing their path were joined by Paul Johnson, a direct descendant of the Edmonsons, and his wife Amy. The Muncaster students' journals, reflections, and photographs from other trips they have taken may be seen on the school's web site (see appendix 1).

The students on the Muncaster Challenge trips have touched, felt, sensed the past by physically moving along the trails taken by people who went before—sometimes even staying in the homes and safe houses used on the Underground Railroad. They are forever changed by the experience.

As Joe Johnson, a Muncaster student I talked with, put it, "On the original Underground Railroad they went from the South to the North to get to freedom. In my personal problems . . . I've been enslaved too, to things like alcohol and drugs, and so I was thinking about how I'm making a journey too, like them."

Joe told me there were times on the simulation he didn't think he'd make it. "What got you through?" I asked him.

"Trust," he said. "Working with teammates. Being able to trust them when I needed help. And I had to trust Mr. Smith and Mr. Durand."

"What did you learn about the original travelers on the path you followed?" I asked Joe.

He gave me facts he had absorbed—facts about Harriet Tubman's life, about the Edmonsons and their journey on the *Pearl*, about Ann Maria Weems, who was only a year younger than himself when she made her bid for freedom. But the things he seemed to walk away with were essentially emotional—a sense of team endeavor, the need to trust others, the understanding that if you do give trust, it will be rewarded, and in turn you will receive trust from others. It struck me that these are powerful stabilizers, healing forces even, for contemporary living, that programs like this go beyond the everyday classroom world of lesson plans and assessment rubrics. The opportunity to touch the story of history so directly is precious indeed.

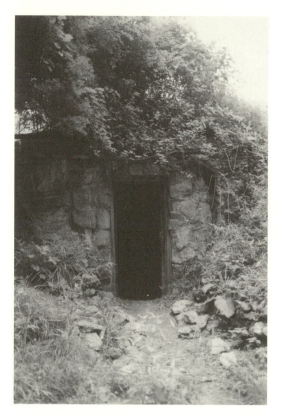

Root cellar where Muncaster
students waited to be told it
was safe to enter their
receiving house, just as thir-
teen-year-old Ann Maria
Weems waited in 1855.
Courtesy of Sally Canzoneri

I asked Reggie Smith, one of the Muncaster staff who has played a
pivotal role in developing this program, "And you? What did you take
away from these experiences?"

"Compassion," he replied, "the compassion we felt on our trips.
People opened up their homes to us—total strangers. These were people who owned historic houses, houses that had offered sanctuary to
people escaping slavery. They treated us like family." If primary sources
are what we're after, there is powerful material to be explored here!

What advice does Smith offer to teachers wanting to embark on a
project like this?

"Be ready to work hard, and I mean really hard. Be ready to form
partnerships. Make sure you have plenty of energy."

Was it worth the work?

Smith laughs. "Well, we're getting ready to do it again!" And he tells me about a student who has been inspired to document his own family's escape, from El Salvador to the United States. The process of following, recreating, and documenting old stories has taken on a life of its own in this school.

When I talked to Vince De Forrest, special assistant to the director of the National Park Service's Underground Railroad Initiative, he mentioned another project involving students studying, and following, the Cherokee Trail of Tears. Clearly there are paths like this across the country, with physical trails remaining to be retraced, and stories of early travelers waiting for students to hear and retell. De Forrest is the Park Service representative who supported the Muncaster trips. He says, "History is prologue. You have to understand it to know about 'here and now.' And historic places, historic journeys, offer a way to do that."

For years the stories of enslaved people remained untold, as the nation struggled first to suppress, and then to come to terms with these unsavory aspects of its past. There are other stories like this, that tend to get left out of traditional renditions of history. They might relate to the place you are visiting and studying—stories of the park, the museum, the historic site, and the way in which it grew to be. Heather Huyck points out, in her 1997 article on the role of women in the West, "Omitting any significant portion of American history distorts all of it. Our history must include everybody if we are to have a history that can help us understand our predecessors and ourselves." In other words, in order to gain a sense of what the prologue to the present is, you have to know the many story threads it contains. Those story threads lead directly to our time, complete with promises fulfilled or unfulfilled, conflicts resolved or unresolved. Huyck goes on to talk about places in the National Parks where the role of women has been examined and interpreted for the public. The Oregon Trail Interpretive Center in Baker City, Oregon, depicts the role of women in trail history. Cabrillo National Monument near San Diego commemorates the sixteenth century Portuguese explorer who claimed California for the Spanish crown, but also interprets the monument's nineteenth century light-house where a woman, Maria Israel, held the job of assistant lighthouse keeper—one of the few paid jobs women were permitted to hold at the time. Look for the presence of women and their history in the story of the place you visit. If it's not there, if it's not interpreted, teach your students to ask questions about its absence.

In recent years, the literary and artistic world has generated thought-provoking material on the subject of women's history. Filmmaker Sandra Pfeifer's award-winning documentary is an example. *Kathryn and Her Daughters* is a film about a seventy-six-year-old widow who raised seven children on a farm during the 1950s and 60s. Hers is a rural lifestyle that has all but vanished today. Pfeifer says, "Kathryn represents the scores of rural women whose lives were devoted to hard work and love. Her life tells us a lot about rural America and fills in the blank that is missing in our social history about women's work." The film is appropriate for grades 5 through 12.

Another useful, and relatively inexpensive, classroom resource can be found in reprints of quality fine art for classroom use (see appendix 1). Art can often be a meaningful vehicle for teaching history, because of the way in which visual images focus attention and elicit immediate response from students. An art history sequence in the classroom is often a good precursor to physically visiting a historic site or museum.

Museums, of course, are places where we can find history encapsulated thematically and interpreted for us. They therefore make excellent backdrops for a place-based educational experience. But as Steven Dubin puts it in his book on American museums, "museums are not sealed in a bubble. What goes on generally in the culture affects how they operate; how they do their work likewise affects cultural activities." Nor is the history of museums exempt from the shameful excesses of the rest of history. One has only to think of the 1897 cargo of "living Eskimos" delivered by arctic explorer Robert Peary for display at the American Museum of Natural History in New York to know this to be true. The long reach of this kind of institutional history is even more poignant when one considers that it was not until 1993 that the last four skeletons of those long-ago travelers were taken out of storage at the museum and flown to Qaanaaq in Northern Greenland to be buried.

Perhaps the real problem is that we tend to teach history as absolute fact, when it is really an ongoing debate over which version of truth is the most complete, the most valid, the most "real." And so traditionally we have encouraged young people to view museums and historic places too from this fixed and unreal perspective of history as an established and undisputed series of facts. Perhaps a better way to look at enduring institutions such as museums and historic sites is as markers on a trail that is still being tended, and in some areas still being blazed! And more and more, the educational departments of museums are interested not only in helping make exhibitions more accessible to viewers, but in finding out how visitors respond to the material they experience.

Using Dubin's framework, think of a museum exhibit you have seen recently or recall clearly. Consider it from three different stances:

First, think about the intentions of its originators. What did those who created the art or artifacts intend to convey? And at a secondary level, what did the curator of the exhibit mean to say in gathering this collection and presenting it this particular way?

This examining of intention is important. Equally important is the realization that this is where we traditionally stop. If we don't teach children to think beyond creative intent, or curatorial intent, they will leave with information only, and without the tools to know how to use it.

Second, consider the social context of the exhibit you are thinking of. This is the "stuff" creators of art and museum objects drew upon in making these pieces. For example, to understand a medieval manuscript illumination, one must think about the social context, the life of the monk in the cloister who made it, why it was made, and who is was for. And one must bear in mind that our knowledge of that life is constantly changing, no longer absolute truth but an ongoing search for greater and greater understanding—an exciting search that with any luck will draw in the future historians and archeologists and ethnographers who stand at those display cases on their third or fifth or seventh grade field trips.

Which brings us to the third and last part of the triad implicit in Dubin's framework—the reception, or what you as the viewer bring to the exchange when you view that exhibit. Audiences come with their own biases, memories, preconceptions, and preferences, all of which shape how they view a place or an object. Young audiences are no different. When I first began working with visiting school groups at Aztec Ruins, I quickly learned that it's possible to live in the heart of Indian country and still view Native Americans in a stereotypical manner. Feather headdress illustrations and princess rescue stories cropped up regularly among the schoolchildren, the product of social stereotyping, far removed from the reality of the contemporary, let alone the traditional lives of Native peoples. Even the Native American kids in the groups were buying into these images. Of course one might argue that my biases lay in quite another direction, but were still biases. I, however, had thought through my opinions in this matter and arrived at a point with which I was comfortable. It did not seem as if anyone had ever asked the teachers, or the kids, where they stood in their perceptions of Native peoples, which ranged from "noble savage" to "downtown drunk."

At Aztec Ruins, our cultural presenters now address this issue directly at each workshop session, simply by sharing their own experiences of present-day Pueblo life, and linking it with the story and art traditions they trace back to their ancestors. The stereotyping of characters in the students' stories has dramatically diminished as a result.

Sometimes museum exhibits stretch the awareness of the public. Sometimes, however, they invoke anger or controversy. There have been many examples of this, from the Smithsonian's *Enola Gay* exhibit in 1995, protested by U.S. veterans' groups as being pro-Japanese and anti-veteran, all the way back to a notorious Metropolitan Museum of Art exhibit of the 1960s in New York. The *Harlem On My Mind* exhibition focused on the history of the cultural capital of black America from 1900 to 1968, embraced photography as art, and was the first audiovisual environment ever created in an art museum. But it aroused widespread ire on all fronts. Critics disapproved of the use of multimedia communications technology in an art museum. Black painters and sculptors were outraged by their exclusion from the show, and the Jewish community condemned the catalog introduction for its seemingly anti-Semitic statements. The exhibition launched the first major controversy in the modern museum world, and catapulted into popular parlance the song title it was named for. A social studies or citizenship class focusing on censorship might profit from a study of such controversial exhibitions and their place in public debate, in connection with a museum visit.

Many schools participate in National History Day, a program that offers an opportunity for young people to use research tools and strategies to investigate historic events, times, and people of their choice, and present their findings in a public forum. History Day was started as a local contest in 1974, and went national in 1980. In 1999–2000, more than half a million students from all states and the District of Columbia took part in the program. For many students, visiting a historic site to study about it should be part of the process of developing a History Day project. Even teachers who do not participate in History Day can draw valuable lessons from the History Day program about how to use historical places, primary sources, and artifacts in their classrooms. (For further discussion of History Day, see chapter 4.)

If you can't take your students on a field trip, look for ways to bring the field trip to them. Some museums will send speakers to your school, and many museums and sites loan out boxes of replica artifacts to schools. Primary source documents, photos, and illustrations are available from many sources, commercial or otherwise. The National Archives publishes reproductions of documents from its collections, as do many museums. Sometimes these come in packs, with related materials and suggested activities. For example, Britain's Imperial War Museum (see appendix 1) puts out a pack on D day that includes copies of maps and orders actually used in the Allied invasion of Western Europe in World War II.

The internet is a treasure trove of primary sources and what is available grows daily (see appendix 1). The American Memory site of the Library of Congress makes a wide range of materials available over the net. The National Archives and the Smithsonian Institution have put virtual exhibits and many primary source materials on the net. Many sites offer both primary sources and lesson plans for using them. A good place to start looking is at the National Endowment for the Humanities site.

CHAPTER FOUR

History Day in Your Classroom

National History Day is not just a day—it's a year-long educational program culminating in a national contest in June. For over twenty-five years the National History Day program has promoted systemic educational reform related to the teaching and learning of history in America's schools.

For History Day, students choose topics related to a broad theme (e.g., Taking a Stand; Triumph and Tragedy; Turning Points in History) and create projects about the topic. Projects can be displays (essentially mini-museum exhibits), papers (either fiction or nonfiction writing), audio-visual projects, or dramas. Students can work individually or in groups, and while they must pick topics within the broad theme, specific project topics are of their own choosing. "Triumph and Tragedy," for example, could mean the end of World War II to one student, the Kennedy years to another, and the civil rights movement to a third. Projects are judged at school fairs, with the winners going to regional, state, and national competitions. At the regional, state, and national

---

Material for this chapter was developed by Sally Canzoneri and is used with her permission.

levels the projects are judged by working historians, and students are interviewed by the judges. Many schools get outside judges for their school fairs as well. Students value the interviews and are thrilled to have adults discussing their work with them in a serious and respectful manner. Revisions between stages of the competition are not only allowed but encouraged. For many students, this is the first time they've had the opportunity to polish a project and experience the rewards of making a piece of their work better.

During the past six years, Sally Canzoneri has worked with hundreds of Washington, D.C. middle schoolers participating in History Day. A broad cross section of students was included: gifted and talented, ESL, special education, children of privilege, children of poverty, and uncategorized just kids. Almost all of them got excited about History Day and found it to be the high point of their social studies course. Almost all wanted to participate again. Moreover, those who succeeded in History Day were not just the "usual suspects." One team Sally took through local and regional competitions, all the way to National History Day, was made up entirely of children who spent most of their time in the special education classroom.

Kids are not the only ones who get excited about History Day. Parents quickly become converts too. They, like the volunteers who judge entries at the national level, rave about how excited, involved, and knowledgeable the children become.

Teachers, though, have mixed feelings. Those who participate in the program think it is a terrific idea as do teachers who do not participate in the program. But teachers worry about whether they have the time and resources needed to start a History Day program and keep it going. If you haven't done it and even if you have, it can be a daunting task. Teachers already face large demands on their time, and the pressure to prepare students for the high-stakes testing that most states now require can discourage teachers from doing History Day, though they may want to.

What makes History Day so exciting and educational? And are there ways that you can bring that excitement into your classroom, even if you can't launch a full-scale History Day program at your school?

When Sally introduces History Day to a class of students who are new to the program, she begins with a story about David Van Tassel, who first launched National History Day. "I want to tell you about a wonderful man," she says. "He was a historian, and like most adult historians he really liked his work. But one day he realized that something awful was happening to kids all over the United States." She pauses. "You know what it was?

"Kids were growing up thinking that history was boring! They thought that history was just about reading dull books and memorizing dull facts and dates. They weren't finding out how much fun it is to be a historian.

"Well, this man decided to do something about it, so he thought up National History Day. The great thing about History Day is that kids get to do what real historians do. And you get to see why they like doing it so much."

She goes on to help the kids make a list of what historians can do in their jobs. These include creating exhibits in museums: writing historical fiction and film scripts, or contributing their expertise to the writing of these; writing nonfiction history; making documentaries or contributing to them; and teaching. Then she explains how, in History Day, students get to do the same things.

One of the mysteries about history education in the United States is that students consider it to be so boring. Yet in the marketplace, Americans young and old love history. Historical books (both fiction and nonfiction) are bestsellers; historical sites and museums are popular attractions; historical themes have always appeared on TV and in the movies. People research their family histories, reenact Civil War battles, and dress up like Renaissance era jongleurs, knights, and ladies—just for fun. History is not boring. It is the story of lives and people, and that is never boring. What is boring is the way we teach history.

Joy Hakim's multi-volume *A History of Us* is a brilliant example of how to speak about history to young people. It was first published for recreational reading. Now, a few years after it came out, some schools have adopted the series as textbooks. Teachers who use it rave about the books. They even have students staying up at night to read their textbook by flashlight.

Hakim writes, "History is a mystery. You gather pieces of information and try to discover how they fit. Suddenly, when you have enough pieces in place, you begin to see the big picture. That's exciting . . . because new pieces of the puzzle keep fitting in."

History Day is exciting for kids because it presents history this way, and it lets students get to work on this mystery puzzle right away. In doing so, they must deal with a whole series of fascinating questions: How do we go about solving this mystery? How do we get the facts? How do we figure out what the picture looks like? How can we be sure the picture we've painted is accurate? How do we tell other people about the picture we see? How do we convince them that our picture is accurate? And how do we get them to be excited and interested in the story we have to tell?

As kids deal with these and related questions, they develop their ability to think critically. They also develop some important academic skills in a situation where they can see the importance of these skills and take pride in their mastery of them. For example, many of the students Sally worked with could recite the definitions of primary and secondary sources, but they could not tell her which kind a particular source was, nor, before they took part in History Day, did they understand why it mattered. Note taking matters in History Day. It is not just something the teacher makes you practice. Students learn to think through and develop theses, to chose carefully the facts and illustrations to make their argument, rather than hand in an undifferentiated catalog of facts. Students learn to work together and to schedule their work so that they can complete the projects on time. They develop skills in written, verbal, and visual communication.

If you want to develop a History Day program at your school, there are a number of excellent resources available. You can find out about these from the National History Day office (see appendix 1). Their web page is a great resource, as are the web sites of a number of the state programs, which are linked to the national page. State coordinators, your key contacts, are listed on the web page. It's a good idea to talk to other teachers who have been in the program. Your state coordinator can provide the names of some near you. A number of respected museums and archives (e.g., the Smithsonian Institution, the National Archives, the Library of Congress, state historical societies) support History Day and provide a wealth of materials. The easiest way to access these is on the web. You'll find links at the National History Day web site.

Staff at museums and historical societies in your area can be another valuable resource, as can faculty in the history departments of local universities. They can help you in a number of ways. They may have collections with primary sources that can be used by your students. They may be able to come to your school to talk to students. They are likely to know historians and history buffs in your area who might want to mentor students or even volunteer to judge at your school fair.

As with so many other school activities, parents are a key resource. They can help you with the administrative aspects of your program; or they can share their expertise with students. Of course, they can work with their own children.

Wonderful as History Day is, there may be good reasons why you are not going to organize a History Day program in your school. You may be working with students who are too young to participate. Some states offer the program for fourth and fifth graders, but most start History Day at sixth grade. Or you may not have the necessary resources and support available. Nonetheless, there are ways that you can bring the History Day approach to teaching history into your classroom. If you do, you'll generate the same kind of enthusiasm for learning history that we see in students who take part in the actual competition. Here are some suggestions on how to give students some of the History Day experience in other activities:

1. Have students visit historic places and work with primary sources and artifacts as much as possible. These are the original puzzle pieces that historians work with to solve the mystery of what his-

tory is. Because they are particular, and not generalized, they are
genuinely more interesting than many secondary sources, especially textbooks. Wouldn't you rather watch the actual game than
just read the report in the next day's sports page? Reading the
report on the sports page makes sense if you have seen the game.
Wouldn't you rather hear a political candidate's own words and
judge him or her for yourself than hear someone else's paraphrase?

Moreover, if students don't experience historical artifacts and
sources firsthand they can't understand much of what they read
in their textbooks. Reading specialists tell us that it is important
for many children to have visual and sensory experiences to connect with words in order to comprehend what they read.
Experiencing historical places and their material culture can give
students this additional context. In some classrooms where Sally
Canzoneri worked, the students were using a popular social studies text which "explained" the Industrial Revolution in four pages.
Most of the sixth graders had never seen a loom or a spinning
wheel; indeed, they had no idea at all how the fleece of a sheep is
turned into a blanket. Not surprisingly, most of them got through
the chapter on the Industrial Revolution by memorizing the definitions and gained no real understanding of the pain, drama, and
importance of this landmark time.

Visiting historic places and working with primary sources and
artifacts also helps students develop their historical imagination.
In order to understand history, we have to be able to imagine
what life was like for people in another time and place. Seeing
actual places and things can help students do this. For example, a
student living in present day Washington, D.C. with its modern
urban transportation system cannot easily imagine why George
Washington would see its location on the Potomac River as a benefit. The student can't easily understand why building canals
seemed so important to Washington and his contemporaries. A
trip to any of the streams, canals, and waterways once used for
transportation all over the country will lead to tree trunks bearing

the scars of old cables used for barges, and well-worn tow paths. Students will then be able to see, hear, and feel the obstacles these barge men needed to get around and to experience how they did it. This kind of exposure can then make understanding the movement of goods, and then commerce in general, and finally basic issues of economy, real and important. A fourth grade girl who wears jeans and sneakers to school can understand the experiences of a Victorian girl better if she has donned a long dress and practiced walking up and down the stairs of a mansion "like a proper lady."

For many students, oral interviews are a particularly good primary source. They put a real human face on events, and make information about other times, gathered from those who are passionate about those times, easier to understand.

2. Provide opportunities for students to tell their stories of history. Every historian makes choices about how to present what has been learned through research and study. The opportunity to make such choices is one of the things that so engages kids in History Day. You can give students this opportunity in the classroom by asking them to create projects using sources you provide or specify. These do not have to be exhaustive projects. Instead they can be time-limited ones that drive themselves because there is a logical end in sight. For example, students can select a topic, write a script, and mount a reader's theater performance (see appendix 1 for Reader's Theater resources). Instead of having students prepare large displays, consider having them present information in the form of a handmade book. Concertina books and origami books are forms that work well for this. Paul Johnson's *A Book of One's Own* offers a wealth of ideas on book arts, and might well inspire outcomes far superior to the standard white display board.

These are the kind of projects that can give you good opportunities to integrate history and language arts. They also fit well

Accordian book and model of the Washington Monument. *Courtesy of Emily Canzoneri*

into a program of performance-based education and can build student portfolios. Moreover, they provide fine opportunities to develop and use rubrics with students.

3. Give students opportunities to publish/display and discuss their work with a respectful audience. The experience of discussing their projects with the judges is one of the things students like most about History Day. Try to give your students a similar experience, perhaps by having readings or presentations to which parents and others are invited. Or put the students' work on display and have an opening. The most important thing is to give the students recognition and a chance to discuss their work. Talk to your local historical society and ask them to help find qualified volunteers who would be willing to look at your students' work and discuss it with them. In History Day, the judges are all volunteers and they regularly comment on how much they enjoy talking with the students.

4. Giving your students access to historic sites and primary sources is easier than you may think. One thing students learn in History Day is that historic sites and primary sources are all around us. Often, students do terrific projects on local history using local sources, or they find a local source about a national event. If students are learning about recent history, their own families, school staff, and other adults they know can be good sources. A wonderful example of this is the book *Oh, Freedom* by Casey King and Linda Barrett Osborne (1997). This book grew out of a project King did with her fourth grade students, who wrote their own personal histories of the civil rights movement by interviewing their parents.

You and your students can look at your town and neighborhood as a historic site. The National Register's Teaching with Historic Places web site (see appendix 1) offers guidance on how to "read" the history of a place in its buildings and lesson plans on teaching with local historic places. The My History web site of the National Endowment for the Humanities offers suggestions on using local and family sources with students.

Some combination of these and many other possibilities might be just what your curriculum needs to get your students so busy unravelling their particular history puzzles they have no time to stop and think about whether this is work and they ought to consider themselves bored with it!

CHAPTER FIVE

In City and Forest

Wild places are both closer at hand and easier to find than one might think. They sometimes lie in officially designated forests, deserts, grasslands, or wetlands. Some of these might even be true wilderness areas, difficult to travel to and not designated for public use or recreation. But the National Forest Service lists recreation as the fastest growing use of public wilderness areas. Although they are now restricted or even banned in selected places, recreation on public land today frequently includes the use of off-road vehicles that can take people to formerly inaccessible places. As a result, the Forest Service began a "Leave No Trace" educational program in order to ensure that recreational use does not result in the degrading of forest ecosystems. Many Forest Service units have an educational coordinator who will gladly link with schools and educational groups to make sure the students' visit to the forest is both informative and enjoyable. Another goal of the Forest Service is the lesser known one of preserving heritage sites—the physical resources located on National Forest lands that offer key connections to the nation's historic and prehistoric past. These resources include the physical remains of prehistoric and historic cultures, places of cultural or religious significance, written records, and oral histories.

This is a goal that also includes public educational experiences and opportunities.

But National Forest land is not meant only for public recreational and educational use. Under the jurisdiction of the U.S. Department of Agriculture, it is designated as multiple use land. Grazing and timber harvesting are permitted in these forests, within federally defined limits. Mining permits are sometimes issued. With burgeoning energy needs pushing public policy toward exploitation rather than conservation of resources, National Forests offer tremendous potential for students to study and discuss issues of ecosystem management and preservation, versus issues of resource exploitation and need.

SAMPLE QUESTIONS FOR DISCUSSION AND RESEARCH IN WILDERNESS AREAS

1. *History of the landscape:* What might this forest/grassland/wetland have looked like 200 years ago? 500 years ago? 1,000 years ago?

2. *Resource use and depletion:* How many board feet of wood does building the average new American home need? How many board feet of wood does one square mile planted with trees yield? How long does it take for trees to mature for harvesting? What would we do if we needed more wood than we could harvest?

3. *Land use vs. conservation:* Whose rights are more important—the farmer's/rancher's/logger's, or the rights of a protected species of animal to wilderness habitat? Is it more important to protect the habitat of a wolf than that of an insect, a bird, a frog, or a fish? Are there ways we can compromise in addressing all these needs, knowing that compromise means the needs of some must be ranked as lesser or greater than the needs of others?

4. *Species diversity:* How many different species of plants can you find in a five-minute search? (Search, photograph or draw,

describe). How many different species of animals and birds pass through here at different times of year? If we cut down one kind of tree completely what might that do to migrating songbirds? Which birds would it affect? What impact would that have on other species (predatory birds or mammals)?

5. *Sensory experience:* How many colors are there in a tree? Look really closely, then from further away, then further still. Write about what you see at each observation point. Smell, hear, touch, and possibly taste (but make sure what you're tasting isn't poisonous).

6. *Evolution of landscape:* What will this forest/grassland/wetland look like 200 years from now? What are the options? What factors will decide its appearance?

7. *Human history:* How many different peoples have used this place? What marks have they left? What marks will we leave? How will we shape what this place will look like in another 200 years? 500 years? What can we do or not do now to make that the image we want?

Wilderness is not only to be found in such nationally designated places. Sometimes a trace of it can be found in the school playground or in the neighborhood. It can be the lone tree on a city street that Kristine O'Connell George celebrates in her collection of tree poems, *Old Elm Speaks*:

> So meek and polite,
> no one knows that
> when all the cars go home –
> when I'm standing here, alone –
> I dream wild. I am *forest*.

Above all, wilderness represents life in all its richness and diversity. Great Smoky Mountains National Park, straddling the Tennessee-North Carolina border, holds such an abundance of plant and animal life that it has earned the United Nations designation of International Biosphere Reserve. The All Taxa Biodiversity Inventory (ATBI) is a research effort aiming to compile a comprehensive inventory of all life forms in the park. It is an intensive project using the expertise of taxonomists, data specialists, biologists, botanists, and ecologists, and volunteers. Once completed, it will provide a baseline from which to measure change in the region.

Volunteers, including school-age children, are beginning to make contributions to this massive data collection effort in the field. Science education specialist Paul Super (1999) reports that students at the Great Smoky Mountains Institute at Tremont, Tennessee, have been monitoring salamander and moth populations. Almost a hundred new species of moths have been identified around Tremont, bringing the known park butterfly and moth species to over 800—an increase of more than 12 percent in one year's worth of work. Ken Voorhis, the institute's director, is hopeful that once the ATBI has been refined for use by teachers, a modified version of it can be used to monitor a variety of species both at the park and in the students' and teachers' own biological backyards. John Pickering, a scientist at the University of Georgia, is working on developing similar projects for school groups to implement—possibly even something as simple as collecting and documenting larvae, thereby providing valuable data on larval stage insects associated with different types of vegetation.

VOCABULARY FOR ATBI USE

ABIOTIC—a non-living factor or element in an environment, i.e., light, water, heat, rock, gases.

BIODIVERSITY—the variety and complexity of species present and interacting in an ecosystem and the relative abundance of each.

BIOTIC—an environmental factor related to or produced by living organisms.

DENSITY—the number of inhabitants per unit area.

DISTRIBUTION—the frequency of occurrence of an organism.

ECOSYSTEMS—the interacting system of a biological community and its non-living environment.

HABITAT—an area that provides an animal or plant with adequate food, water, shelter, and living space.

MICROHABITATS—a small habitat within a larger one in which environmental conditions differ from those in the surrounding areas.

PHENOLOGY—the science dealing with the influence of climate on such annual phenomena of animal and plant life as budding and bird migration.

TERRESTRIAL—growing in or living on the land.

ATBI IN YOUR SCHOOL

An All Taxa Biodiversity Inventory (ATBI) can be carried out at your school to discover what lives in your community. Why is it important to inventory every living thing at your facility? To inquire, to explore, to decipher, to identify, to compare and contrast, to calculate, to classify, to monitor—in other words, to be inquisitive, to ponder, to be scientists.

The following National Science Education Standards are touched upon in these activities: unifying concepts and processes (measurement and explanation); science as inquiry (recording and reporting); life science (populations and ecosystems).

Here are the objectives. The students will:

- determine every living species inside a plotted area;
- observe the relationship of organisms in a particular community;
- consider the biotic interaction of the organisms with one another and with the abiotic factors of the area;

• observe the relationship of soil quality and amount of sun and water for the plot.

Small groups of four to six students each will need:

• four meters (about thirteen feet) of string
• four wooden stakes
• hammer
• containers
• trowel
• magnifying glass
• notebook and pen
• field guides for wildflowers, insects, trees, edible wild plants

Find several areas on your school grounds that won't be affected much by other students. Attempt to have several different ecosystems and microhabitats. Make sure some are next to the school building, some near water, some shady, some sunny.

Measure off one square meter using the wooden stakes as corners and the string as boundaries. If possible, make these plots semi-permanent, so that your students can return to them to see changes due to seasons, weather, and man-made conditions.

Observe the visible members of the community within and estimate their number.

Collect one sample of all different living things within your boundaries. Draw them and describe coloration, shape, and other characteristics.

Using your trowel, dig in one corner of your plot, just under the surface, to discover all the living organisms that exist in the soil. Document/describe the type of soil and the organisms either in words or with drawings. For species easily identified, return them live to their home after studying them.

If you cannot identify something with a field guide, document it (describe it, draw it, even photograph it, or collect a permanent specimen) so that you will be able to check in the future if it's ever been seen before. You can then give it your own name, or you can send it to an expert to identify.

Think about the following:

- What is the dominant species of your ATBI meter plot? Why?
- Describe the characteristics of the populations in the plot including density and distribution.
- How do habitats differ depending upon plot conditions— sunny/shady; dry/wet; protected/trampled?
- How has the plot changed over time? In one week? In one month? In one year?

Reprinted by permission from Great Smoky Mountains Institute at Tremont, Tennessee. Internet, http://www.nps.gov/grsm/tremont.htm

The important thing here is that using the ATBI is not a simulated activity, but a real field experience resulting in the acquisition of real data similar to the kind collected by researchers. The idea behind its original development was to enable data from area schools to be provided back to the institute. But in order to make this possible, a common protocol and database system need to be devised to ensure that the data collected and documented by school and community groups is valid and meaningful. Ken Voorhis of the Great Smoky Mountains Institute anticipates running teacher training sessions once the program begins to take shape, but emphasizes that extending the use of the ATBI to schools close to the park, and collecting resulting data from those schools, is still very much a pilot project. The training sessions will equip teachers to use the ATBI and related materials, and perhaps to develop spinoff programs and teaching materials of their own. That way, schools can monitor the ecosystems in their own backyards in a way that is close to the professional monitoring of these systems on public lands.

At Chaco Canyon, an ancestral Pueblo site in the northwest corner of New Mexico, adjacent to the visitor center and in its trademark dome housing, stands a 25–inch telescope, a gift to the park from a group of amateur astronomers from Albuquerque. Chaco boasts of near-pristine clear skies—there are few city lights around to obscure the views of the heavens. Standing here, watching the sweep of the Milky Way overhead, it is easy to understand why the Park Service is working to get the night sky in this area declared a natural resource.

Both tourists and school groups coming to camp at Chaco get treated to a visual extravagance of star-studded night sky; then to breathtaking views of celestial objects through the telescope; and finally to photographs of galaxies and planets taken at the site. Chaco is turning out to be a modest research facility in its own right. Interpretative specialist G.B. Cornucopia says, "What we have here is definitely a facility that can be used by students. We have made connections with schools and teachers all across the country." Teachers from as far away as Allentown, Pennsylvania, have brought students out to Chaco to observe, and to collect data.

Concern in the last few decades about the quality of science education has led to numerous resources being available to teachers, and many of these resources can be put to use in a place-based program. A major clearinghouse is the National Science Resources Center (NSRC). The Center is operated by the National Academy of Sciences, National Academy of Engineering, Institute of Medicine, and the Smithsonian Institution, to improve the teaching of science in the nation's schools. The NSRC collects and disseminates information about exemplary teaching resources, develops and distributes curriculum materials, and sponsors outreach activities, specifically in the areas of leadership development and technical assistance, to help school districts develop and sustain hands-on science programs. While their focus is not on teaching in relation to place, they offer a wealth of materials and curriculum links that can be tailored to the needs of your place-based project.

A much more modest endeavor, PUMAS (see appendix 1) is an online site hosting a collection of one-page examples of how math and science topics taught in K-12 classes can be used in interesting settings, including everyday life. The examples are written primarily by scientists and engineers, and are available to teachers, students, and other interested parties via the PUMAS web site. The site states the goal is to capture, for the benefit of pre-college education, the flavor of the vast experience that working scientists have with interesting and practical uses of math and science.

Clearly, science offers valuable tools to help young people explore natural spaces both terrestrial and beyond. But the arts have their own tools and techniques, and they too can simultaneously instruct and delight.

Art and ecology are intimately connected. Art educator Cynthia Hollis (1997) speaks of the need to develop ecological art curricula to help reframe the way we think about the earth. She suggests enlarging the boundaries of art education to explore the borders of interaction of people with nature. Artists have long used materials from nature—pigments and dyes for paints, and to color fabric; stone for sculpture; and clay for pottery. Paintings, pictographs, and petroglyphs made by ancient peoples in many parts of the world give us glimpses today of their interpretation of the world.

Some art made today in the outdoors, however, is not meant to endure that long. Andy Goldsworthy, an English artist living in Scotland, builds environmental art with ephemeral objects in nature—branches, leaves, grass. He builds walls with river rocks. He creates striking collages of leaf against bark, snow against earth. His work is transient, blowing away in wind and rain. Studying photographs of his sometimes massive, sometimes delicate, often startling work can provide ideas for young people to use in interacting with the materials of wild places and using them to create art.

Today some artists explore the ways in which people increasingly influence place with buying, consuming, and land-use choices. Exhibits such as *Art from the Global Scrap-Heap*, (sample material from a museum-developed teacher guide, appendix 2) introduce ideas about industrial by-products and their use in creative recycling around the world.

Beginning over twenty years ago in Seattle, planners have sought to

Rock Snake by Shannon Waller's third grade class, Country Club Elementary School, Farmington, NM. Students watched a slide show of Andy Goldsworthy's work, then assembled their snake. *Courtesy of Northwest New Mexico Arts Council*

incorporate into public landscapes art-work that interacts in some manner with environmental forces—wind, water, or sun, for example—to make its impact on the viewer.

In Farmington, New Mexico, visitors to a city park in the heart of a multi-use commercial district are greeted by a giant set of three metal stands topped with rotating mobiles. The sculpture, called *Wind Forest,* is the first of a series of seven pieces planned for installation at various points along a riverwalk. A series of four cross-curricular educational activities involving the sculpture is currently being tested by elementary teachers.

OUTDOOR ART MODEL: *WIND FOREST* ACTIVITIES FOR ELEMENTARY STUDENTS

Kindergarten to second grade

- Watch the mobiles. What makes them move? Do all the pieces always rotate in the same direction? Move like the mobiles, in place, moving with the breeze.
- Back in class, create your own cardboard and wooden dowel versions of *Wind Forest*.
- Collect words that come to mind when you look at *Wind Forest*. Use them to build a group poem.

Third to fifth grade

- Before the visit: Find out the wind speed and direction for the day from your local weather report, on the radio, television, or online.
- On-site: Count the number of rotations per minute of each piece in *Wind Forest*.
- Back in class, create your own models of sculptures capable of responding to wind. Try different kinds of materials, see what might work best. Use an electric fan to try out simulations of different wind speeds and directions.
- Write a poem. Give each piece in the installation a character, and build a story around them.

Sixth grade

- Sketch *Wind Forest*.
- Correlate wind conditions for the day with speed of rotation. Build models using different sizes and shapes of cups, different angles of positioning the spokes, from the ones the artist chose.
- What would happen if the installations were horizontally instead of vertically positioned? Or placed at an angle of 45° to the ground instead of an upright 90°?
- What other ways can you think of to build art by the river,

Wind Forest by Lyman
Whitaker, a wind-driven
art installation, Berg
Park, Farmington, NM.
*Courtesy of the City of
Farmington*

where the pieces interact with the environment? Think of examples using water, sunlight, or the trees. Think of pieces that
might offer spaces for the local wildlife (deer, birds).
• Design two additional art pieces that the city of Farmington
might consider commissioning.

These activity suggestions are intended to serve as a model for
activities related to outdoor spaces where art has been added to the
landscape—sculpture gardens, environmental art installations, even a
single piece of art in a city park. Of course, interactive art like this is
ideal, but much contemporary and abstract art lends itself well to such
cross-curricular thinking, where analyzing material and construction
offer a slant different from the artistic and interpretive.

Whatever your opinions on the urgency of environmental issues, few people today would dispute the existence of degradation, and of conflicts between human and environmental matters. Children worry about these complex issues as adults do, except they feel even more powerless than most adults to do anything about them. When they are given tools to express themselves, what children have to tell us on such issues can be clear and direct, a call to action. Art of all kinds can offer invaluable tools to help make this possible—to help young people explore global concerns that nevertheless have local and immediate focus.

River of Words (ROW) is one of those interdisciplinary projects with local meaning and global implications. Launched by poet laureate Robert Hass, and sponsored by the International Rivers Network and the Library of Congress Center for the Book, it is an annual poetry and art contest on the theme of watersheds. "Everyone," runs the program description, "lives in a watershed. They come in all shapes and sizes." Materials considered in the competition must come from young people from five to nineteen years old, who are not in college. Submissions can come through schools, nature centers, libraries, museums, clubs, and so on. Individuals may also enter. Competitors may submit as many entries as they wish. The only rule is that the poem and/or art must be original, and must be related in some manner to the theme of watersheds. River of Words aims to help young people "discover their ecological address."

The ROW national competition can be a catalyst to get teachers and students thinking about the water systems within which they live. There are many possible levels at which to approach a ROW project, depending on resources and time. All but the most basic involves integrating one or more field trips into the experience. After all, it makes more sense to write and create art about water while you are actually sensing its presence, rather than in the classroom. The International Rivers Network offers a teacher's guide, contest guidelines, and suggestions for using the project as a vehicle for building community partnerships. Such partnerships—with local clubs, businesses, civic groups, and community artists and writers—are not essential, but the wider a

net you cast with this project, the larger the audience that hears or sees
your students' work, and the greater will be the social and community
impact of that work. River of Words can be a single child's work, or it
can be a far-ranging community project celebrating and calling attention to the watershed within which a group of students live and learn.

RIVER OF WORDS: PROGRAM ALTERNATIVES

- Poetry contest only. Children write poems and create art about
  rivers and watersheds in the classroom, and submit their work
  to the contest. No field trip.
- Poetry contest + field trip. Children write on the trail and edit in
  the classroom. They create begin creating art-work on the trail
  and complete in the classroom. Some ecostudies instruction is
  offered on the trail.
- Poetry contest + field trip + writing residency (writer is invited
  on field trip, guides poetry writing, writes and shares own work
  with students). Some ecostudies content is offered before the
  field trip and on the trail.
- Poetry contest + two field trips + writing residency. Ecostudies +
  social studies content (history and culture of the peoples who
  have used the water system), poetry writing and sharing.
  Reading either outdoors, or in a nature center, or back in school.
- Four-month riverine studies unit, with poetry writing, art, and
  science components + two or three field trips to collect water
  samples for monitoring and study. Reading either outdoors, or
  in a nature center, or back in school.
- Year-long riverine studies unit, with poetry writing, art, science
  and social studies components, and multiple field trips to collect
  water samples for ongoing study. Service learning component,
  watershed cleanup. Data gathered is submitted to area government organizations (e.g., city or county councils). Reading and
  sharing all genres of written work, both scientific and artistic.
  Publication of work.

If writing and creating art are ways to foster links between children and nature, children's literature offers a foundation of information and insights on which to build such active learning. But the numbers of children's books published each year are staggering. If you're going to be visiting an herb garden, for example, what is the perfect book on the medicinal use of plants, or the history of ethnobotany? Author-illustrator Lynne Cherry has an answer. Her Center for Children's Environmental Literature publishes a newsletter called *Nature's Course*, offering resources for teachers who seek to use children's books (as opposed to textbooks, or in addition to them) as a part of an environmental studies curriculum. The quarterly publication offers book reviews accompanied by related classroom activities, and includes additional lists of teacher resources.

Native American perspectives often add another dimension to the interpretation of natural places. Joseph Bruchac writes in *Who Says?* about work he has done with the National Park Service to develop a stronger storytelling component for park interpreters, using Native stories to explain the history of their parks. In many cases the park employees who do the telling are themselves Native American. The National Association for Interpretation now includes a Council for the Interpretation of Native People (CINP), whose aim is also to integrate Native American points of view into the ways in which parks are interpreted for the benefit of visitors. CINP's goal is to develop techniques for communicating the heritage, concerns, and views of native people both within the organization of the parks, and in communication with the public.

Storytelling offers a profound and imaginative tool to help young people connect with wilderness. The story resources of Native American peoples underscore these connections because they form such an essential part of Native traditions and world views. Bruchac sees story as a circle, to be spoken of not just in one voice but in many, in a discussion that is continuing. This story metaphor links naturally to the continuing circles, or cycles, found in nature.

Jim Bruchac (Joe's son), who himself wears the varied hats of author, storyteller, and wilderness guide, offers workshops to people of all ages and levels of competence through the Ndakinna Wilderness Project, a program he has developed and nurtured in upstate New York. Jim draws on his own Abenaki heritage and on his sense of the beauty of the wilderness, as well as on tracking skills honed over years, in sharing places special to him with visitors.

To explore a natural place in your area, consider the following:

1. What is the objective of the field visit?

2. What will its outcome be?

3. What kind of expertise do I need to tap?

4. Who can I contact to get the information needed for pre-visit instruction?

5. What reading can I do before I go? What pre-reading can my students do to prepare themselves?

6. What tools or equipment are needed? Do I know their use? If not, can I learn and provide direct instruction or will I need an expert in the relevant field?

7. What follow-up activities will make this trip part of the curriculum rather than an isolated event?

The answers to these questions will dictate the kind of field experience your students will have, what they will study, and what knowledge they will be able to return to the natural setting in which that study took place.

Chapter Six

Using Special Abilities, Accommodating Special Needs

With the coming of age of the inclusion movement and the passage of the Individuals with Disabilities Education Act, the likelihood that the average field trip will include students with identified disabilities is high. From the point of view of equity in education, inclusion makes ample sense. It might sometimes appear to present a few logistical challenges, but there is no doubt that with some creativity and a little effort, the participation of all can make for an experience that is truly beneficial for all.

The following story was related by a Girl Scout leader:

> I had a troop consisting of ten fifth grade girls. They had been together since first grade. One of the girls had multiple disabilities. She had difficulty walking, could only respond with a yes and no, and had some cognitive disabilities. When the girls were younger it was easier to include her. But in their fifth grade year I noticed that when Kathy would try to get their attention or be included, usually by walking or standing next to the girls, they would ignore her or sometimes go so far as to push her away. I noticed she was becoming quite withdrawn and even crying

sometimes, and knew I would have to do something about the situation.

I called the girls together and started describing one member of the group without naming her. I told them, "One member of our group has been feeling left out lately. She feels like she is picked on quite frequently and it makes her really sad. A lot of the time, she feels like she has no friends." I described how this made her feel at some length. Then I asked if anyone knew who this person was. Seven hands rose. I expected each of them to say Kathy, but instead each of the girls who raised her hand said it was herself. Here I was thinking that only a kid with a disability could feel that way, when in fact, most of the kids in my troop had these feelings. As a group, we were able to figure out strategies that would help us to feel better about getting along with each other. The changes we made that day helped not only Kathy, but every child in my troop!

There's something to be learned from this, given that in a far-from-perfect system, in order to receive services, students with disabilities must first be labeled, and their labels often precede them into classrooms. Kids with disabilities are kids first—the scout troop anecdote underscores this poignantly. Keeping this in mind helps when planning, organizing, and carrying out activities on a field trip, and in setting up follow-up activities. We call disabilities by many names (e.g., cerebral palsy, epilepsy, spinal cord injury, blindness). Most of these are clinical or broadly descriptive tags that carry little functional meaning. Disability labels by themselves do not tell us much about how a person can function in a specific environment.

In his book on outdoor education programs, (1993) Stuart J. Schleien and his colleagues offer the following guidelines for adapting activities in these contexts:

1. Adapt only when necessary. Don't use a particular modification only because you have purchased the equipment already, or are

familiar with its application. Assess the activities you have planned. Assess the individual's ability to perform them. Then adapt, if you must.

2. View adaptations as temporary and transitional. Work toward normalizing the activity to the extent possible. Canoeing instructors might begin in a pool, but the most normalizing setting for this activity is out on a lake or river.

3. Adapt on an individual basis, not on the basis of disability classifications.

4. Adapt for normalization. If an individual needs modified equipment, keep it as close to the standard version as possible.

5. Adapt for availability. Training an individual on specialized equipment that is not available or useable on the trail or in the field is a waste of time. Use your judgment to decide what level of adaptation is practical, user-friendly, and non-discriminatory.

Sherril Moon suggests thinking of the following factors when planning recreational activities for and with young people with disabilities. I have used her categories here, adapting each to the needs of place-based teaching*:

Choice. In general, offer the same choices of focus and subject matter to your students with disabilities as you do to those without. Sometimes just being in a place that offers stimulation, being part of an experience that feeds all of the senses, will push the boundaries of what we think is possible with some students. If choosing is a problem, then by all means help narrow the choices, offer options, but to the extent possible allow the student to select and follow what is of interest to him or her.

---

* Adapted with permission from Moon, M.S. (Ed.) (1994). *Making school and community recreation fun for everyone: Places and ways to integrate.* (pp. 6–10). Baltimore: Paul H. Brookes Publishing Co.

Age-appropriations. Modify the process, not the age-level of the outcome. Simplify the project if the student is cognitively unable to understand it, but never scale it down to materials or techniques that only a
much younger child would use. A teenager with mental retardation is
nevertheless a teenager.

Family involvement. Family members can often provide invaluable
assistance on field trips, helping to keep the group together, taking
small groups in separate directions, and so on. Plan with family members of students both with and without disabilities exactly how you
propose to utilize their help. That way, the student with a disability
does not have to be singled out for this attention, but can feel part of a
larger group. This is all part of developing support systems referred to
as "natural supports." Those in the immediate environment, whether
young people or adults, can offer the most natural and often the most
commonsense accommodations, in an unobtrusive and therefore
acceptable way, without the student in question needing to feel pin-
pointed for "special assistance."

Professional roles. Moon discusses the role of the therapeutic recreation
specialist here. In the context of teaching in public places, special education teacher-consultants, audiologists, reading specialists, are all professionals whose skills can be drawn upon to make the field trip and its after-
math an experience of worth for the student with a disability. Classroom
aides and even peer helpers can be used in the support system.

Leisure education. This relates to an area most of us would describe as
"quality of life"—as measured, for example, by what we do with our
free time and what interests we choose to pursue. Place-based education exposes all young people to a wider range of ideas and opportunities than the same content taught in the classroom ever would.
Learning about the growth of the railroad in a West Virginia museum
with a steam locomotive exhibit not only brings the period to life, it
offers students models for both career and recreational opportunities.

I know of high school students who decided to volunteer at a small regional museum in their senior year because of such a trip. That was a significant leisure option they would not otherwise have known about.

Physical fitness and motor skills. Clearly both outdoor and indoor place-based education can offer opportunities for fitness, and gross motor and fine motor activities. Outdoor activities in particular affect aerobic and motor capacity and reduce weight—clearly something as important for people with disabilities as the rest of us who are "temporarily able-bodied."

Partial participation and adaptations. According to this principle, even though some people with disabilities might not be able to function independently in a given situation, they should still be able to take part to the degree possible, with assistance when and where needed. If everyone else is working on a model or a poem or an experiment, your student with a disability must do so too—although perhaps with assistance, or with physical modifications, or even with modified outcome expectations. Of course, reasonable accommodation should only be made when a need exists. If an individual with a disability wants to try an activity without accommodations, he or she should be encouraged and supported.

To Moon's comprehensive list I will add this. We must know abilities, but we must not allow our students to be restricted by our perceptions of their limitations.

I once went on a field trip to a park by the river with a group of second graders and their teachers. We walked down a trail, then stopped at a bridge to write. One child, unable to resist the temptation to test gravity, threw a piece of paper into the water. I let him know the point of this trip was to write about the river and not throw things into it. I can be an environmental fanatic when I'm aroused. I tried to keep my voice calm but my face must have registered my disapproval. The

teacher took me aside and explained that Charlie was a special education kid, and perhaps he just didn't understand.

I wasn't quite sure what to do next. It was Charlie who carried this
moment forward. He said, "Okay. I'm sorry." He brought out another
sheet of paper, and began to work. He stopped only to ask, "Can you
help me because my spelling's really bad?" I told him I didn't care how
he spelled just now because we could always fix that later. I asked him
to put down the best, most wonderful ideas he could find, in a way that
would make sense to him when he read them out. Among all the kids
who wrote that day, Charlie was one whose poem sang, and I am certain he responded differently to the juxtaposition of trash and water
the next time he encountered it.

Including students with physical disabilities on a field trip often
necessitates a prior survey of the site, as well as of the personal accommodations a student regularly uses or might need to use at the site.
Assessing this can include considering a number of reasonable accommodations. The following table offers a range of assistive devices and
accommodations for people with disabilities.

ACCESSING RECREATION

ASSISTIVE DEVICES/ACCOMMODATIONS FOR PEOPLE WITH DISABILITIES

Ambulation
- **paving**—should always be smooth and free from debris
- **curbcuts**—should comply with ADA* and be free of snow and
  standing water
- **barrier-free pathways and halls**—no standing objects (e.g.,
  couches, garbage cans) that could make the hallways narrower
- **handrails**—must comply with ADA guidelines for height; make
  certain they are securely fastened
- **wide doorways**—must comply with ADA guidelines; applies to
  all doors (e.g., classrooms, bathrooms), not only front doors

---

* ADA—Americans with Disabilities Act

Grasping
- **lever doorknobs**—operated by the lever handle rather than a round one
- **gripping gloves and straps**—these can be found in many catalogs or can be created from Velcro, Dycem, and/or Scoot Guard
- **built-up handles**—handles and controls made thicker by using tape, wood, or other materials
- **Dycem/Scoot Guard**—both are rubbery materials to prevent slipping; can be used, for example, as a placemat to assist in holding papers in place; Dycem is costly and can be found in therapy catalogs; Scoot Guard can be found in hardware stores
- **Velcro**—can be used to hold items together or to hold hand to items

Vision
- **barrier-free pathways and halls**—no standing objects that could make it difficult to navigate (e.g., if someone is using a wall to navigate, a sofa could be in the way)
- **controlled noise level**—too much noise can be disorienting; use dampening materials in large, noisy areas
- **contrasting colors**—directional and informational signs (including restroom signs) should be printed in contrasting colors; the best is yellow on black, the worst is a lighter shade of one color on a darker shade of the same color (e.g., light blue on navy blue)
- **large print, Braille, cassette**—all program information (from brochures to guided tours) should be available in all three formats; large print is fourteen points or larger
- **sighted guides**—staff should be available to assist individuals to get around facility and to describe sights, where appropriate (e.g., exhibits), and the layout

Hearing
- **TDDs**—Telecommunication Device for the Deaf, a device that allows the person to type instead of talk on the phone

- **FM Units/loop systems**—both devices can assist individuals to hear
- **ASL, PSE, CART, Oral**—all types of interpretation; before hiring an interpreter, identify which type is necessary for the individual
- **written materials**—whenever possible, provide voice materials in a written format (e.g., a booklet instead of a cassette-guided tour)

Cognitive
- **verbal instruction and demonstration**—give instructions verbally and through demonstration; make certain an individual understands what is expected by asking him/her specifically (not just the whole group)
- **pictorial language**—utilize pictures wherever possible (e.g., arrows, pictures on signs)
- **rule adaptation**—modify the rules where necessary
- **modify entrance criteria**—allow a less advanced individual to participate in a more advanced group so he/she can remain with peers (e.g., swimming lessons)
- **utilize natural supports**—encouraging group support

From *Don't Forget the Fun: Developing Inclusive Recreation,* reprinted by permission of the Institute for Community Inclusion, Children's Hospital, Boston.

Some students with disabilities might require assistance on a field trip with activities of daily living (ADL)—eating, dressing, toileting, and personal hygiene. The scheduling of such activities should be discussed and agreed upon with the individual or parents/guardians, to allow time for them as needed, and to allow the group to adjust for that time. Pay attention to such factors as site access (Is the bathroom accessible? Do the others in the group know not to inadvertently block or impede access?); toileting (What specific assistance is needed? How much extra time is needed? Is there special equipment the child needs to use and care for, such as a catheter?); eating (How much assistance is needed with food preparation and feeding?); and other personal care (dressing, brushing teeth, or preparation for sleep, in the case of overnight experiences). Students with cognitive disabilities might need reminders or checklists. Many have systems for these tasks already in place at home, so then it is just a matter of making sure they transfer that skill to a new setting.

The McGill Action Planning System (MAPS) is commonly used in creating a long-term plan for and with an individual with a disability. It is a transition strategy that helps parents, educators, peers, and the child with a disability to plan collaboratively for the future. Including the child with a severe disability in place-based learning experiences might necessitate the inclusion of field staff at the site to be visited—the nature education program, for example, or the wilderness camp, or even the museum education center.

The MAPS process consists of seven questions asked of the child and/or parents and family members, and related to the following areas:

- History
- Personal dreams, worst nightmares. Questions in this area are aimed at building a picture of the child for teachers and other team members.
- Strengths, gifts, and abilities
- Needs
- Ideal day (at the place to be experienced), and what must be done to make this happen.

MAPS offers a set of directions for team members to support the student and integrate him/her into school and community life. For a teacher including a child with a significant disability in a place-based program, a simple review of the questions, whether or not it is accomplished through a formal meeting, can help identify roadblocks and develop the necessary modifications or detours to either overcome or avoid them.

For those who wish to examine more closely the issues, challenges, and rewards of integrating outdoor education, and in particular wilderness programs, to include persons of all abilities, Stuart Schleien and colleagues (1993) offer conceptual frameworks, resources, and suggestions for administrative and systemic change. A chapter in their valuable resource book on outdoor education is devoted to activity plans and curriculum materials ranging from fish prints to canoe touring.

For students with disabilities, the involvement of families in the planning process when getting ready for an out-of-school learning experience is critical because in order to provide appropriate school and community services, one must first find out exactly what they and their families want and need. Sometimes this can involve teaching families what their rights are, or teaching them how to advocate for their child, or letting them know what services they can reasonably expect from the school system. Often this relates to issues of dependence versus independence with which both the student and his/her family are struggling. In all of these circumstances, student, teacher, and family must be a team. In place-based education they must talk to each other about more than the logistics of the field trip.

Cooperative rather than competitive activities in all phases of a place-based learning program will make for more authentic and participatory learning on everyone's part. Such activities also offer students with disabilities a chance to contribute their strengths to the process rather than be hampered by their limitations.

On a wilderness hiking trip, toting their gear to the trailhead, a sixth grade class split into two groups, one going ahead of the other. Coming to a fork in the trail, the first group worried that if they went on, the others might not be sure which way to go. One of the group, a boy who used crutches and could not carry more than a backpack, offered to stay at the fork and direct everyone. Carrying the gear, it became clear, was not the only important task that needed doing.

A focus on needs and tasks, while important, should be balanced by consideration of the individual strengths students with disabilities, like all other students, bring to a field experience. Sometimes, it is in fact the child who sees the world differently from the rest, who is in the unique position of being able to offer insights to others. The student with a psychiatric disorder might not always be socially appropriate in how she expresses these insights—but it does not mean she does not have them, nor does it mean they are not worth sharing. Variability in sensory and cognitive perception can often offer unusual points of view to those of us who do not have the label of a disability. Students who see the world in eccentric or unusual ways can contribute to the understanding of the story of a place in a fresh, creative manner.

Parks and museums often contain their own stories that relate to disabilities and their impact on all of us. Often they are hidden, as are women's stories, or stories of people of color. When students find such narratives in their inquiry about a place, they are taking part in a process of knowledge-building, both for themselves and for the community to which they present that newly acquired knowledge. The example that follows is from Colorado, but many parks and museums have similar stories.

In San Juan National Forest near Mancos, Colorado is a broad, pleasant half-mile trail called "Big Al." Al is Al Lorentzen, a San Juan National Forest employee injured while working as a firefighter in 1988 on a fire near Yellowstone. He and another crew member had been sent into a "hot" area by their section boss. A partially burnt tree fell, trapping Lorentzen and severely injuring his spine. He has used a wheelchair ever since. Over the years, Al Lorentzen has worked as a consultant, helping the Forest Service design campgrounds, picnic areas, and offices that are accessible to people with physical disabilities. He no longer works for the agency, but the trail that bears his name is testimony to his energy and enthusiasm for opening wild places to people with physical disabilities. The Big Al trail leads through oak brush and aspen stands, and wildflowers, out to an overlook that offers a breathtaking view of the river below and the mountains beyond. It is a trail frequently used by school groups and families. A signpost offers visitors brief background information on the construction of the trail, and on the man for whom it is named. What was meant in this case to be a reasonable accommodation for visitors with disabilities has clearly brought benefits to everyone.

CHAPTER SEVEN

Stewardship and Curatorship

When students write at Aztec Ruins they can never think about the place or its associated people, past and present, in quite the same way again. As one fourth grader put it, "This place is special to me now. This place is MY place."

Whether the goal of a site or institution is preserving habitat or taking care of a cultural resource, the key to its continuation as a valued part of the community lies in its ability to foster in the next generation a sense of stewardship. You can only take on the role of caretaker of a place if you feel a vested interest in its preservation and maintenance.

There is an alarming number of incidents across the nation's parks in which the foolish and foolhardy behavior of people has resulted in damage and loss to life and property, and to sites we count among our national treasures. Despite posted warning signs, people insist on doing things like petting bison, feeding bears, and throwing trash into streams and rivers. They pick up artifacts and rocks from historic sites as souvenirs. They even break into parks' premises and vandalize buildings. They fail to dress or prepare appropriately for hiking and mountain climbing, costing enormous sums of public money in rescue efforts. The single biggest fire in Yellowstone's disastrous 1988 season was a 406,359-acre inferno, caused by someone tossing a cigarette butt into the tinder-dry forest. Teaching our children to cherish these places and care about their preservation is not a luxury we can postpone.

The Junior Docent Program at the Palm Springs Desert Museum in California is an example of stewardship in action. Here, twenty-five high school students at a time are trained to serve as junior docents for specific exhibitions. Letters are sent to educators to recruit young people for the program. Students recommended by teachers or administrators complete an application form and go through a selection interview. Once picked, they must sign an acceptance agreement, a commitment to be present for both training and tour days for the duration of the program. A summer institute format is used for training, with a dual focus: intensive exposure to content related to the exhibit, and communications skills needed for taking on the interpretive role of docents. Following the training, the young docents work at the museum one morning a week for ten weeks, giving tours to fourth and fifth grade students. They also get class credit through their schools for participating in the program, a family membership to the museum, a $200 stipend, and a certificate of merit upon successful completion. Most important, they leave with a feeling of commitment to the museum, knowledge of a part of its collection or exhibition, and an enhanced understanding of its place in the community.

Stephanie Harvey, a Denver-area educational consultant and author of *Nonfiction Matters: Reading, Writing, and Research in Grades 3-8*, suggests that in the context of writing instruction, and in particular while teaching nonfiction writing, collection and assimilation of knowledge is something to be celebrated. One element of Harvey's model dovetails neatly with the purposes of museums and historic sites—the personal curatorial collection.

Human beings are collectors. Each of us has a personal treasure trove of ideas, objects, books, music, posters, related to one or more subjects about which we are passionate. In a sense, all knowledge derives from this kind of curatorship. When you feel strongly about something, whether that something is skateboarding, feathers, or ancient Mayan architecture, several things happen quite spontaneously:

- you collect information about your passion;
- you generate questions about it;
- you collect objects, artifacts, and images related to it;
- these in turn generate further questions;
- you seek out sources of information to answer those questions.

You become, in fact, a curator and custodian of your collection, asking and answering questions, interpreting the facts you accumulate, organizing your knowledge in order to make meaning for yourself. This is the beginning of all inquiry.

Now here's the wonderful thing that gives this very common trait particular meaning for the elementary classroom. Most parents will relate to the experience of trying to separate thoroughly laundered remnants of baseball cards, stickers, or leaves from the gummed-up pockets of jeans and jackets and T-shirts. This of course is because people between the ages of eight and twelve are in the happy phase of just having discovered the marvelous human propensity to imitate the pack rat! Teachers of young people in this exciting developmental phase of discovery of world and self ought to capitalize on it.

Harvey suggests beginning a sequence of nonfiction study by discussing the role of a museum curator—in particular the curator's ultimate purpose of making collections meaningful and accessible to others. She suggests building a community of learners by capitalizing on the expertise every child has, on a subject each feels strongly about. A bulletin board for sharing information becomes a mechanism for students to serve as resources for one another. At the elementary level this might be a space entitled "Just So You Know." At the middle grades it might be a two-column chart, "Information Available" and "Information Needed." What the teacher is doing here is setting up the right conditions for children to explore their own interests. This will foster the asking of serious questions, and will therefore be likely to lead to serious efforts to find answers to them. No one, argues Harvey, can ask questions about something of which they know absolutely nothing.

A central part of this kind of nonfiction inquiry is the modeling by the teacher of the research process—and not just the kind of simulation modeling that teachers use frequently to offer examples or demonstrate concepts. No, here the teacher actually conducts an inquiry of his or her own while the students do the same. So if students, for example, are researching a wide variety of subjects, from dog behavior to Irish ghosts, the teacher is simultaneously bringing in and sharing her ongoing research into, say, the lives of pioneer women. As the children share their ongoing triumphs, frustrations, and progress, so does the teacher.

Because the teacher is modeling the development of a "real" project, students get to see two important aspects of the process of study:

1. That a work in progress is allowed to be imperfect; and

2. That the process of revision is often uneven, requiring much revisiting and repetition.

This, by the way, is a very important idea—that the first time you think and write about a subject, what you get is no more than a rough draft. It is also mostly an unpalatable idea to the average middle grader, who is likely to dash off a "report" and declare it "done." But in the end, abiding interest in a subject can turn repeated revision and rethinking into a fascinating endeavor rather than a tedious chore.

Setting up the right conditions for serious research is only the first step. You then have to show kids how to go about finding answers, and then how to organize that material into something coherent, capable of being shared with an audience. Teachers engaged in nonfiction inquiry teach the steps of the research process, model those steps, set up the

Next page: *Ecosystem at Its Finest* by Stephen Dibben, Corey Jensen, Erin Abernathy, and Kelly Draper of Wyoming, all age eleven (1993, mixed media). See Chapter 10 for discussion. *Courtesy of David Cowan/Greater Yellowstone Coalition*

conditions for the production of work—and then release responsibility for that work to their students. In the context of place-based teaching, what this involves is the following:

1. Choice in the subject to be explored.

2. Clear expectations about the final product of that exploration. If you're writing a field guide, you have to read lots of field guides, and find out the difference between those that work and those that don't.

3. Tools to work with. For example, if you're measuring the acidity or alkalinity of water samples, you have to know what materials to use, how to use them, and how to record results.

4. Books to read. If you're analyzing the impact of a painter's life on his work, you have to know something about both, beyond what you see in a gallery. If you're writing about Thomas Alva Edison and the light bulb, you must read both biography and science history. You must also know how a light bulb actually worked in Edison's time, and the changes it has undergone since then.

SHOWCASE OF PERSONAL CURATORIAL COLLECTIONS

Content Area: Language arts + content area relevant to each collection

Skills: Knowledge, comprehension, application, analysis, evaluation

Strategies: Observation, discussion, decision making, research, writing, classification

Duration: 2–3 hours a week, beginning 4–6 weeks prior to museum field trip

Objectives: In their study of their personal collections, students will:

1. Select, classify and sort objects and materials related to their collections.

2. Research additional information pertinent to their collections.

3. Present selected exhibits from their collections.

4. Write and present a nonfiction piece on the subject of their collections.

Materials: Tables to display collections, as owners share them; pencils, paper; construction paper and index cards for exhibit signage.

Vocabulary:

CURATOR—the person in charge of a museum or art collection.

EXHIBIT—to place on show (verb); an object or collection of objects that is shown (noun).

Teacher Preparation: Bring your own collection in and share it with the class. Discuss curatorial collections and invite students to talk about the things they collect. Begin writing about what they will be presenting later on. Write five to ten minutes a day, either free-writing, or using a simple K-W-L format (what I know, what I want to know, what I've learned), until each child has decided what to exhibit.

Procedure: Set aside time each day to develop collections, research questions. Students should keep a notebook to document what it is they know already about their subject; what they wonder about; topic lists; quotes; observations; interviews; research notes; bibliographic notes; beginning drafts. Notebooks should have pockets to hold printouts, postcards, photographs, and other visuals they might want to incorporate into their presentations. As the children develop their presentations, they will:

• gather information;

• decide what to present;
• decide how to present both objects and information;
• write about their passions;
• assess their collections in progress, offering and soliciting feedback regularly.

Set aside time each day to share the collections in progress. Share
your collection in progress, and write about it, modeling the procedure
for students. Finally, the week before the museum field trip, schedule
presentations of the collections to the entire class. Presenters will read
their nonfiction pieces and share objects and related material from
their collections. The collections may be left on display for a specified
length of time, and the rest of the school, or selected classes, invited to
view them.

A museum visit, part of a place-based learning sequence, offers an
opportunity for students to begin developing, organizing, and sharing
their own collections, and in addition, beginning to see them as works
in progress. Behind-the-scenes visits with curatorial staff can sometimes yield remarkable insights into the continuing evolution of even
very large museum collections.

If you want to integrate ownership of a place-based educational
project into an entire year's curriculum, you might be interested in
investigating the Scottish Storyline Method (for contact information,
see appendix 1). Here teachers and students use the power of story to
create a setting and characters. Plot in the story evolves as real problems
are addressed and the content unfolds. All Storyline units involve more
than one area of knowledge and skills. Here is a brief list of the content
areas covered in Jeff Creswell's (1997) description of a Storyline project, "Underground to Canada," created in response to Barbara
Smucker's book of the same name:

• literature (trade books on the subject, fiction and nonfiction)
• astronomy (people escaping slavery were guided by the
  stars)

- history (the slave trade, the abolition movement, escapes and rebellions)
- music (spirituals)

The Storyline method of teaching, in which the teacher folds all instruction into a series of topical questions about a central story (in this case the story of people escaping slavery) can bring a place and its story into the classroom in a way that children can understand and process.

Another example Creswell details is a unit founded in language arts goals, which involved creating a radio station. He wanted the children to learn about writing for a specific purpose, and he wanted them to learn to edit their writing for a clearly defined presentation. Subsidiary goals were improving observation skills through drawing, and learning the criteria used in designing a logo, as well as minor goals in career education and science. Using an actual vacant building in a commercial district as the proposed site for the radio station, the class began to make their plans. In the process, attempting to do more than merely build a simulation, they were introduced to the harsh realities of the real estate rental market. Despite the frustrations that came from finding out about the $3,000 annual rent, and the realization that no bake sale could possibly raise the money needed for such a small business, they did build a beautiful mock-up radio station in the classroom and selected a name, KPIC, or Kids Put In Charge.

Selecting logo designs provided yet more real-life experiences, of determining practical criteria for selection, and realizing that what looks grand in color might be muddied considerably in black and white.

At each stage of the process Creswell raised questions for his class—each guided by the overarching question for each phase, "What do we need to know?" In the end, the children produced and recorded a real radio program. They made several practical discoveries, such as the real-time length of three minutes. And (a magically culminating presentation) they visited a real radio station, run largely by high school students, and were interviewed by them. The interview was taped, and listened to back in the classroom with all the trepidation and excitement, says Creswell, "of anxious families gathered around the radio listening to Churchill announcing the end of the war." The connection to a real place was a broad loop that came back full circle in this project, and there can be no doubt that process and outcome were owned and cherished by each child who took part. The underlying objective of all place-based teaching was clearly met here.

Creswell's use of story as the heart of instruction sometimes offers ways to connect to the very immediate environment in a very tangible way. A few years ago he did a Storyline unit on "The New Playground," in which the children designed a new playground for the school. They worked with a parent in the school who happened to own a playground equipment company. They conducted whole school surveys, and concluded the topic by presenting their design ideas to a PTA meeting. Their enthusiasm and expertise helped launch a playground committee. This in turn resulted in the development of plans to build an actual new playground at the school in the summer of 2000. The "real" playground was directly inspired by the work of the children.

The parent who owned the playground equipment company in Jeff Creswell's anecdote could certainly be termed a stakeholder—someone with an interest, concern, share, or investment in this process.

Teachers of course are always stakeholders in the instructional process. But they are not the only ones. Here are some obvious others:

- students
- families
- school administrators

And here are some perhaps not as obvious:

- school board members
- park or other site staff
- the larger professional and geographic community, including representatives from chambers of commerce, businesses, and nonprofit arts, educational, or cultural organizations

- other cooperative agencies (libraries, historical societies, nature conservancies, land-use groups, any other groups with specialized knowledge or resources to share)

The National Park Service, in providing a framework for assessing its Parks as Classrooms programs, recommends making sure that data is collected from stakeholders after the completion of a program, so that this feedback can be utilized in revising and refining interpretive and educational outreach work. Teachers who have been most successful in incorporating the resources of a site into their own instruction have done so by identifying the stakeholders early in the process and using multiple human, organizational and material resources to meet program goals.

The following guidelines are helpful in developing the kind of learning experience that will lead to a sense of responsibility for the site you are learning in and about:

Choice. Not only allow but require choice in the area to be studied; this will lead to more authentic inquiry, and allow multi-modal learning to take place because students will naturally respond to those cues from the environment that feed their idiosyncratic learning styles. Within the structure of all successful programs we are likely to find plenty of opportunity to follow individual interests.

Individual differences. Select the means of exploration in light of the abilities and talents of your students. If you keep in mind the variety of learning styles you are dealing with, and accordingly guide students toward information and materials, you will be stretching both their interests and their capacity to use that information meaningfully.

Social learning. Offer opportunity for social learning to take place. Nothing strengthens a sense of connection to place more than having it reinforced by the interests and energies of a peer group. Make sure students are given the opportunity for some open-ended interaction at the site, sharing observations or reinforcing each other's newly acquired knowledge.

Affective learning. Solicit the kind of feedback that leads to affective learning—voicing an opinion, drawing an original conclusion, expressing a feeling or a point of view. In this kind of forum, there is no right or wrong answer. The teacher merely asks what students think or feel about a place, accepting all responses as valid. This is not to minimize the importance of knowledge acquisition, but to complement the cognitive with the affective processes of gaining understanding.

Organizational tools. Provide the tools for preparing that knowledge for dissemination. Sometimes this might be as simple as offering ways to organize materials, or construct a logical report, or write a letter. The content and complexity will vary with the project.

Cooperative learning. This differs from social learning, which is spontaneous and often occurs incidentally, during planned activities. In a cooperative activity, a task is set and the group plans and executes it, and evaluates the outcome. This kind of task-focused group work can often be a means to developing and planning (and then reviewing and assessing) the culminating event that will serve as capstone to the entire process.

Chapter Eight

Taking Outcomes Back to the Community

Knowledge and understanding of most educational content are greatly enhanced by the process of communicating that content to others. We do this in the adult world through papers and conferences, workshops and seminars, theatrical performance and dance, articles and stories and works of art. Each unit of place-based instruction must include some forethought about how students will convey what they learned to the following arenas:

- the school community
- the wider community
- the place where the field experience occurred

To some extent the scope of the culminating outcome activity will determine both the product to be developed through the field experience, and the activities to be included in the experience itself. When the product (whether poem or field guide, play or dance or story) is to be presented to an authentic audience with a genuine interest in its content, the process of creating it is spurred by the same kind of urgency that prompts adults to work to real deadlines for real projects. When children work hard with me on their stories at Aztec Ruins, it isn't because I say so. It is because they know their work will be on display for all to see. They know that tourists from as far away as Germany and Japan might see their art and read their stories. They know that's so because they have flipped through the guest book where those tourists sign their names and leave their remarks. And they know they will wear a clip-on microphone, sit under a spotlight, and read to an audience that might include some people they do not know. The product and the need to complete it thoroughly and well thus assume a tangible significance far exceeding any grades that might be earned along the way.

How an outcome event will be structured will depend on what you, individually or in consultation with your project stakeholders, decide the final product of your place based experience will be. Whether students end up writing poetry or collecting environmental data, telling sky stories or compiling a report on the documented presence of native plants versus invasive weeds, it is important to hold some sort of outcome event that will both present their work and offer cause to celebrate it publicly.

There are several kinds of outcome events that might serve as the culminating activity of a place-based learning process:

- A reading of work produced during the experience. This is particularly appropriate if the writing is fiction or poetry, but it also works if the students wrote trail guides, or reports, or even letters. An intergenerational project might, for example involve young people sharing collected items from a nature walk with residents of a senior center; or interviews of seniors by students for a history project, the outcomes shared at a reception honoring the participation of both groups.
- An art exhibition, with a reception honoring the young artists, as well as any resident artists who might have taken part. Sonja Horoshko, the artist I worked with at Aztec Ruins, who has conducted numerous residencies with young people in schools and in park settings, emphasizes the need to display the work in a

professional way, with titles and bylines and wall text about the work and the artists.

- A museum exhibit of objects and work by students, hosted by the site where they focused their study. In keeping with the idea of a professional presentation, this gives the site a curatorial function relative to student work. It creates a lasting, institutionalized bond between young people and the sites they study.

- A walk through a trail or museum exhibit with the park superintendent or museum educational director, using a trail or exhibit guide developed by the students. Such events are smaller in scope, and might perhaps be appropriate for team projects in which a smaller number of students have worked together rather than individually.

- A storytelling event, focusing on stories read or told by the students

- A brunch, dinner, luncheon, or tea, complete with speakers and dressy clothes and ceremony, as formal or informal as you choose, but featuring presentations by the students

- A campfire event

- A professional paper presentation by students, using formats and conventions of the field of their study

- A dramatic or musical performance

This is by no means a comprehensive list. The possibilities for outcome events are limited only by your imagination. Some will be obvious, given the projects students have worked on during and after their field experience. Others will need greater planning. How you go about this depends entirely on your time, energy, people power, and ideas!

However varied they might be, most outcome events can be cooked up with a few basic ingredients:

Collaborators/stakeholders. Businesses, educators, families, site-based staff, and kids can put together a wonderful event if everyone works

together and at least one person (possibly you) keeps in mind the grand
plan of what the event will encompass. Assemble your team carefully
for this culminating event. Delegate tasks, by all means, but hold fast to
your vision, and make sure that everyone working on this agrees on the
basics of what is to happen. Find collaborators in the larger community
outside your school. Perhaps the local public library is interested in
bringing an outreach van, with booklists and handout materials relevant to your theme. Perhaps the local literacy council would like a
stake, and will then be willing to offer volunteer or material help. Or a
museum or nature center might want to use your event as a forum to
launch programming of their own.

Funding. It is expected that the site will provide the place for the activity at no cost, but you will need to clarify all aspects of this ahead of
time. If the entire process was collaboratively planned and executed
(i.e., so that the site and its personnel feel included, and do not function merely as setting and props) this should be a natural outcome, but
it's always good to make such things clear from the outset! You might
need to come up with money for extras such as food, certificates of
appreciation or participation, and transportation. Sometimes local
businesses will be happy to sponsor an event such as this, or underwrite
the costs of displaying or publishing student work, since sponsorship
will get their name onto all publicity and commemorative material,
and earn them community goodwill. Again, check with the site to make
sure there are no restrictions you should know about. For example, federally run sites, including National Parks facilities, are not allowed to
accept any donations that carry overt advertising. I learned this the
hard way. Even if an ice cream company wants to donate refreshments,
you might have to turn them down because their name-brand labels
can be construed as advertising. If your state department of education
offers teacher mini-grants or "dream grants," your project might fit
their guidelines. Or your local PTA, arts council or philanthropic foundation might see it as a small project worth funding. At a minimum,
local businesses are usually good for in-kind donations of refreshments

or gift certificates. Make sure you acknowledge all in-kind donors in publicity and program materials. That is not advertising—it is a goodwill gesture.

Publicity. Send out flyers to parents, friends, school board members, community leaders, anyone else who was involved in the field experience, and those who think they'd like to be involved next time. Send press releases to radio and television stations, and newspapers, especially school, local or community papers.

SAMPLE PRESS RELEASE

FOR IMMEDIATE RELEASE   Contact: Ann E. Enthusiast
Phone: 101–111–3333
Email:annenthused@anywhere.org

Children Present Dramatization of Historic Event

The Anytown Museum is pleased to host a performance by third graders from Anytown Elementary, on Thursday, March 25, 2005, at 6:00 P.M. They have worked with teacher Ann Enthusiast and with museum educational staff on designing props, and on directing and producing the performance, which is based on the current exhibit, "Miniatures in Five Traditions." The children wrote the play when they toured the museum two weeks ago.

The performance will take place at the Museum's Little Theater, and will be followed by a reception. The event is open to the public, and is free, although there is a $3 fee for adults who wish to tour the museum exhibit. Refreshments for the reception are courtesy of Anytown Bagel Factory.

Please bring your family and friends and celebrate the work of Anytown Elementary's playwrights and performers.

Additional venues for disseminating findings. Local bookstores and libraries are often happy to display art and science projects, or post information about your event. An indoor mall might be willing to do a one-time display. Malls might even let you set up a table to display student work, and at the same time seek public donations to put into the pot for next year's program, if you in turn acknowledge their permission to use their space as an in-kind donation.

Online dissemination. If your school has a web site, it is a natural place to post not only information about the event but about the entire field experience and even perhaps the art, writing, and findings of students, along with links to the web sites of all organizations and people who were in any way involved with the project. Space on a web page offers you the opportunity to acknowledge those you haven't had a chance to thank in person, and to publicize the linkages you established so that others seeking to replicate your project will gain some ideas on how to do so.

Outcome events crown your program, but if you hope to do this again next year, you have to carry out a few basic follow-up tasks. At their simplest, these might be a handful of thank-you letters to the organization hosting your field experience; to sponsors, funders, parents or family members who helped; your principal or school board; media people who helped publicize the event; and any other community supporters. If you have run a successful first event, and want to repeat this in years to come, follow-up might involve some research on funding sources to expand or enrich the program, or simply to ensure it can take place again.

Evaluating your experience is a necessary and often very enlightening part of your project. Evaluation could be as simple as connecting with your stakeholders and asking them the following questions:

What worked?

What didn't?

Should we do this again?

What would you want us to do differently?

Who else should we involve?

ANYTOWN ELEMENTARY/MUSEUM COLLABORATION PROJECT

Please take a moment to fill out an evaluation form for us. We'll use your feedback to help us make future programs better.

1. Is this the first Young Players Performance you have attended?
   ☐ Yes   ☐ No

2. What did you like about the performance? About the program that led up to it?

   _____

   _____

   _____

   _____

3. What would you like us to change/improve?

   _____

   _____

   _____

   _____

4. Any suggestions for future programs of this nature?

   _____

   _____

   _____

   _____

This program was made possible by generous support from Anytown Museum and Anytown Bagel Factory.

Sometimes it is appropriate to make up a brief evaluation form and request families and others who attend a culminating event to complete it and return it to a box on the way out. See page 99 for sample form.

Finally, make sure that when you carry out any kind of formal or informal evaluation, you check with the people most involved with the project—your students. Too often program evaluations neglect to ask participants what they thought. If students have forged the kind of links with place you meant them to establish, they will probably be more than willing to share their opinions with you so you can make this work better for other groups in the future.

Chapter Nine

State and Local Resources

Not all of us have a designated National Park, or a registered historic site, in our backyards. Despite that, most of the ideas discussed here can be implemented in whatever natural or historic site is near you. Every place has its own stories to tell.

Often these stories are encapsulated in small museums, both publicly and privately operated. Lynne Arany and Archie Hobson have compiled a list of over a thousand of these small (and not-so-small) American showplaces. Their book, *Little Museums,* is organized by state, and includes an index by category. It is well worth a look, to see what kinds of museum collections might lurk unknown to you in your neighborhood. Dayton, Ohio, for example, boasts a state memorial to Paul Laurence Dunbar, who worked as an elevator operator in this town. Later, the African-American dialect poetry he wrote from his experience as the son of former slaves gained him fame. Corpus Christi, Texas, has an International Kite Museum; Watertown, West Virginia showcases America's first kindergarten. The size and scale of these "little museums" vary greatly. Some are monuments to regional or local passions. Others represent the eccentric imagination of a single individual, or the hoarded contribution of a family to the nation's cumulative attic.

There are gems waiting to be explored in this collection of "little museums" and some might offer outreach programs. Yet others might welcome adoption by a school service project, to help maintain grounds, publicize collections, or lobby for greater support for development or preservation. And still others might be appropriate long-distance resources for a unit of study that extends the notion of community beyond geographical boundaries (see chapter 10).

Sometimes families can offer remarkable resources. Attics and basements often house collections with their own history and sense of place. Linking families with local museums, or even using an internet resource such as My History (appendix 1), can lend a whole new dimension to the study of a community's history and its place in the American experience. Families might include scientists or historians or collectors who might be willing to come in and lend their expertise to a stream walk or an evening stargaze or a museum visit. Or they might include seniors willing to share the valuable oral histories they hold in memory. Find out who the families of your students are, and learn to honor their gifts and abilities. Arts and crafts, foods and the particulars of material culture, stories and writings and trade skills to be found among family members—all can be pulled into a place-based project, time and space permitting.

State departments of tourism often have valuable information about places whose natural beauty or historic interest they use to draw tourists into the state. Most often, if they are places worth a visit by out-of-state tourists, they are certainly worth exploring by young people who live nearby. Tourism department materials are often geared toward the recreational uses of these places, but can provide a basis for educational use as well. Dams, lakes, state parks, state historic sites, memorials, wildlife preserves—each of these can serve as setting for your place-based activities. Wilderness areas under state jurisdiction can often also provide resource personnel, materials, and outreach activities.

The North Carolina Division of Parks and Recreation offers an environmental learning experience booklet for each state park and recreation area. Each booklet contains activities to be carried out before, during, and after a visit to the park. All activities are correlated to the state's instructional competencies. Material in the booklets is multidisciplinary, and geared towards experiential learning in the parks. It serves as a model for teachers, as well as park personnel, who might be interested in developing such materials in a different setting.

Urban environments sometimes offer valuable and unexpected green spaces. In Toledo, Ohio, the Park-It! project was designed in 1997 as a multi-faceted effort involving the use of city park land for land laboratories; providing native trees and wildflowers for planting within the land labs; providing workshops for teachers; providing reference library materials to participating schools; and writing and distributing curriculum activity guides for use by teachers. Sites measuring an acre (3,920 square meters) for each of five land labs were selected in a process involving neighborhood public information meetings. Split-rail fences were erected around each site, and a special dedication ceremony marked the planting of eleven native deciduous trees and an array of native wildflowers. Oversight for each site was to be provided by a committee made up of representatives of faculty, staff, and students from participating schools. Curriculum guides address a wide range of learning objectives across the K-6 age range, in the four broad areas of soil, water, plants, and animals.

Subsequent to the inauguration of the project in 1996, one school altered a gate and widened wood-chip paths to accommodate students in wheelchairs. Three of the original five schools are still managing the land labs. One never got off the ground, because the focus of the school changed from magnet to charter, staff changed, and there was no follow-through on the project.

Park-It! ran into management and maintenance dilemmas that would be wise to consider when designing similar programs in your community. School principals changed since the inception of the project. Teachers moved on. When personnel changes were accompanied by administrative changes in school organization and structure, the land labs suffered. Wildflower flats delivered by the city were not planted. Weed growth overran native plants. The handful of teachers who use the land labs consistently and with care are at this time overshadowed by the number who do not. And as always when land use is involved, developers and others in the neighborhoods are beginning to eye some of this land for uses unrelated to education.

Marilyn du Four, a city employee who was involved in designing the Park-It! land labs, points out that a project like this is not an expensive proposition. Fencing and tree purchase are the main initial expenses. Seeds can be collected. Naturalizing occurs on its own.

In hindsight, it seems as if the major problem with the Park-It! project is not its design and conception, but the fact that teachers were not involved from the inception. Some teachers who were asked for feedback on the curriculum guides suggested they would have been interested in helping from the start, perhaps even helping develop the guides. In return for students maintaining the land, and learning from it, the city offered a wealth of in-kind resources and technical assistance. To assume that schools citywide could sustain interest and enthusiasm in the project was perhaps too optimistic. That this did not happen suggests that it is people and not systems that make progressive, creative programs happen. Systems are essentially reactive, responding to the latest educational mandate, trend, or crisis. Learning occurs when knowledgeable and enthusiastic people interact with each other in places that hold meaning.

Park-It! still remains a pilot project worth scaling down and replicating within other communities, perhaps using space within school grounds, or as a collaborative effort between a single teacher or group of teachers, and a single city park or other local government or private organization (civic groups such as Kiwanis and Lions are possible partners).

The city of Toledo parks offices continue to be inundated with requests for their curriculum activity guides from places around the state and beyond. Staff are willing to provide information on the project to those interested in developing sites such as this in their ecological backyards (see appendix 1 for contact information). The guides are applicable to urban and suburban school curricula and habitat type across Ohio. Although they focus on Eastern plants, wildlife, and ecology, the format is easily adaptable for use in other geographical areas, substituting local plant and wildlife information while maintaining the overall focus on stewardship and resource management.

Any discussion of green spaces raises questions that have to do with resource use and management. Educators and youth specialists at the Idaho Water Institute (see appendix 1) have developed curriculum materials for use in grades six through nine, using issues-investigation methods to develop an awareness of a wide range of waste management concerns. Students can explore how concerns become issues; identify waste management concerns in their communities; explore the range of options and opinions surrounding a local waste management concern; and develop and carry out a community action plan. The Environmental Management Power (EM*Power) curriculum developed at the Institute is action-oriented and experience-based. Six consecutive lessons use games, role plays, interviews, teamwork, and related activities to develop the analytical skills needed to explore and address complex issues. The developers of the curriculum suggest that making a difference can take many forms: cleaning a stream; conducting wide energy-use campaigns for home or school; establishing or refining recycling programs; stenciling storm drains; or adopting a highway or stream. The curriculum materials can be adapted for use with younger children.

Other community resources worth considering in building local networks are scout troops, outdoor education and skills programs, and Boys and Girls Clubs. Across the country these community groups offer an immense array of programs and facilities—photography labs, camping programs, wilderness exploration, and community service projects, to name a few. They are generally interested in forming connections with local education agencies and with individual teachers to the mutual benefit of all.

Small and large businesses with a presence in your community are additional resources to consider tapping. In the American story, businesses from steel to ice cream have left imprints upon the landscape and the imagination. Factory tours figure prominently on the itineraries of visitors to places ranging from Seattle to Hershey, Pennsylvania. Additionally, newer companies seeking to market innovative practices or those with socially conscious agendas often welcome connections with schools and young people, and are willing to offer their premises for tours and more. Tom's of Maine, producer of natural toothpaste and other personal care products, has regularly offered tours of the factory to small groups. In response to community interest, the company now offers outreach programs for grades K-3. Matt Mooney, who handles outreach at the Tom's of Maine headquarters in Kennebunk tells me he and his colleague go into classrooms, and demonstrate toothpaste making with the kids.

"In class?" I ask. "Can you do that?"

"It's like baking a cake," he assures me. "We can do everything except a mild heating process we use at the factory, but basically it's mixing and stirring." And he lists ingredients: calcium carbonate, hydrated silica, glycerin. . . .

Even though we're talking on the telephone I feel as if I'm beginning to smell the company's trademark mint and strawberry extracts! Mooney says they are in the process of designing programs that will work for older students as well as the early grades, focusing on the chemistry of toothpaste manufacture, or the dilemmas of environmental ethics.

The model at Tom's of Maine seems to be working. There are dialogues waiting to be started with other businesses, perhaps even some in your community currently seeking ways to connect with schools. Pick the ones whose products and business practices you feel will provide positive models for your students, or whose stories offer insights into your study of your own community.

Sometimes place-based programs might need additional funding support. State educational agencies or arts commissions might have resources to offer those teachers who are interested in developing nontraditional collaborations, and willing to do some grant writing to support their programs. Many states have public art programs—infrastructures set up to place installation art in places frequented by the public. Some are turning now to using arts residencies with working artists as the medium for placing such art in the public eye. Check with your state arts agency (appendix 4) to find out the public art policies that govern such programs in your area. Statewide funding sources both governmental and private might offer program development options worth exploring, depending on the content area you are interested in connecting to your place-based program. If your population includes a diverse socioeconomic group, state welfare-to-work programs might offer small pockets of arts or enrichment funding for residencies, or for parent/child after-school activities. State departments of education can often provide information and contacts for these options. The Foundation Center (see appendix 1) is an excellent source of information on private foundations offering grants to educators and those with whom they forge partnerships.

In the private sector, corporate giving strategies can also sometimes mesh well with the needs of schools. It is best to begin by familiarizing yourself with the charitable contributions priorities of the business you are considering approaching. (No point applying to a business for a science-related program if all they will fund is music or sports.) Then make a reasoned decision about whether or not your program fits the company's priorities. Each company is likely to have different cycles of giving, eligibility requirements, and application procedures. Begin with a telephone call or letter requesting information on each of these areas. Businesses in the area of technology development or infrastructure, for example, are likely to be interested in supporting place-based programs that offer a technology instruction or usage link.

Taking stock of your local resources is a good place to start, and it's something you might want to do periodically as you design and implement your place-based program. Keeping a simple checklist and updating it as you progress can be make this task considerably simpler and less overwhelming. See page 108 for sample form.

For very young children, the familiar and commonplace can be exciting places for "behind-the-scenes" visits. A kindergarten teacher I know makes it a point to plan an annual class field trip to her house.

PLACE-BASED PROGRAM

Site name and address:_____

Phone number:_____

Site contact person:_____

Fax:_____

E-mail:_____

Stakeholders	Tasks	Commitments/in kind	Funding
Collaborating teachers	☐	☐	☐
Principal	☐	☐	☐
Families	☐	☐	☐
Site-based staff	☐	☐	☐
Students	☐	☐	☐
Businesses	☐	☐	☐
City/county officials	☐	☐	☐
Online publishers	☐	☐	☐
Funders	☐	☐	☐
Others	☐	☐	☐

Her students tour the house, sample mint tea in the backyard, and draw maps—of the house, of the neighborhood, of the path to the doghouse.

For students at the other end of the age spectrum too, there are often numerous state or local learning opportunities that lend themselves to place-based teaching. State legislatures welcome visits from young people when they're in session, and if students are visiting because they are interested in tracking a specific piece of legislation related to youth or child welfare or the environment, then the visit becomes purposeful. Education staff at zoos can sometimes offer opportunities to learn about large animal veterinary medicine, or captive breeding programs for endangered species.

Whatever the age or abilities of your class, wherever you live, there are treasure troves waiting to be explored in your backyard. And don't stop with the few suggestions in this book, either. As Arany and Hobson put it in *Little Museums,* "Who knows what gems lie behind other, unopened doors?"

CHAPTER TEN

Learning at a Distance

Much of the material in this book has focused on the need to physically sense a place, explore it, and study it through that exploration. However, there are some significant exceptions to this model. Far from detracting from the importance of the kind of experiential learning discussed so far, these options in programming might actually expand the reach of major public sites, to bring them within the grasp of geographically distant people and communities. Sometimes this occurs through special programs, such as the Yellowstone project described in this chapter. Increasingly such connections can be forged electronically. This chapter presents some models for distance learning about place, with or without the field trip as part of the experience.

Individual parks often have their own reasons for launching educational initiatives and seeking collaboration and participation from far-flung communities. From 1988 to 1995, Yellowstone National Park sponsored an arts program for school-age students across the country. The program was called iMAGiNE! Yellowstone. Themes were selected for students to focus on: Fire; Wild Things Are Welcome Here; From Geology to Landscape; and Endangered Species. Young artists used a multiplicity of materials and methods. They absorbed information,

110

asked questions, and created art, both individual and collaborative, that was striking in imagery and varied in form. More important, the art integrated in many thoughtful ways both the place they were considering and the content they had explored and discussed. That places, like people, are not static, was dramatically highlighted at the very outset of iMAGiNE! Yellowstone. The first participants heard about the project just before the 1988 fire season. What was originally visualized as a one-year celebration of the park through student art and writing grew into a "significant regional forum for young people's perceptions of wild land on fire" (1997, Blandy and Cowan).

Thomas Moran, the well-known Rocky Mountain School painter, imagined Yellowstone in a series of woodcuts made for an article in *Scribners Monthly* (1871). Similarly, students were asked to respond to Yellowstone themes in ways that were both personal and creative. Background was provided by a student/teacher guide and slide program, informational brochures, and various research papers relevant to a particular year's theme. Though many teachers brought their students to Yellowstone as part of the park's resident environmental education program, or participated in the park's Moran Artist-in-Residence Program, visiting the park in person was not a mandatory requirement for participation.

I contacted David Cowan, one of the creators of this project, and asked him how it all worked. "Students could participate in fourth through twelfth grades," Cowan wrote in reply. "Once a student participated, he/she would be mailed all pertinent materials for subsequent events until graduation. Some one hundred teachers also participated annually. Many integrated the project into their classroom units on ecology, parks, wildlife, conservation, geology, endangered species, etc. Every year I advertised the project with science and art councils, teacher associations, museums, and schools throughout the country.

"Though I talked with many participating teachers on a regular basis, reminding them of the project goals and the need to provide guidance in a light-handed manner, the heart of the project was in the classroom. All media and styles were acceptable, I would tell teachers

Painted Wolves by Erin Baldry of Montana, age twelve (1992, tempera). *Courtesy of David Cowan/Greater Yellowstone Coalition*

and students, as long as the creation was an expression of your personal response to the theme, and didn't require a Mack truck for delivery to Yellowstone." Paintings from this project can be viewed on pages 84–85, above, and 114.

The 1990 iMAGiNE! Yellowstone exhibit, *The Wolf,* featuring selected work submitted by students across the country, hung at the Denver Museum of Natural History. An exhibit catalog was published, filled with lush and beautiful images and words of children, imagining America's first national park. In Cowan's afterword in the catalog he tells of families visiting the museum and coming upon the exhibit. Children are drawn to the display, awestruck in the presence of work by other children. And he tells of the wonder of tactile connection! Crisscrossing the gallery, the children touch the caption plate of each piece, absorbing the young artists' names and where they live, eyes fixed all the while on the piece of Yellowstone Park that hangs on the wall.

Following its spectacular initial success, the iMAGiNE! Yellowstone project was shelved for administrative reasons. But the ideas it generated have stayed and grown into other projects, including an Artist-in-Residence program. Yellowstone, the place, traveled miles with this endeavor, its community uninhibited by the boundaries of physical space.

The conversations and e-mail exchanges I had with David Cowan gave me insights into the way individuals with vision can shape the boundaries of their own communities. To my delight, David felt that the interest of people like me in iMAGiNE! Yellowstone, people who had heard about the program, or seen the traveling exhibition of the art it produced, bolstered his own belief in the program and its worth. That, after all, is one definition of community—people with ideas in common, working toward shared goals. Technology being what it is, programs not in geographically contingent places can now go beyond trying to do the same thing in different settings—they can offer support, assistance, and technical resources to each other.

As I write this, I am happy to report, the iMAGiNE! Yellowstone program has been revived. For the past five months students in Bozeman, Montana secondary schools have been studying and responding to issues and themes related to the Yellowstone River. The students are still working on their artistic creations. The river will be a continuing theme for two years, and a summer program aims to weave expressive art activities into a Lewis and Clark expedition simulation with young people, following rivers that flow into the Missouri.

The virtual world certainly shares one aspect of iMAGiNE! Yellowstone—limitless reach. In the realm of writing, "virtual residencies" are gaining popularity, providing ways for students to connect with writers far from their geographical vicinity. The Johns Hopkins University, as an adjunct to the programs it offers to gifted and talented students, provides mentorships with university graduate students in

Burnt Night by Meagan McPhie of Wyoming, age twelve (1991, chalk). *Courtesy of David Cowan/Greater Yellowstone Coalition*

math for middle and high schoolers enrolled in a distance learning course.

Clearly e-mail can be a powerful connecting tool. But it might appear at first glance to offer little potential for programs trying to link students with the very things the medium itself seems to be dismantling—physical places, and real-time activities taking place in them. Might a virtual program related to a real place be an oxymoron, after all?

Last year I was contacted by a teacher in a part of New Mexico about five hours from where I live. She had attended a workshop at which I spoke, where she had heard about the work I was doing with teaching in and of place. She wanted me to come work with her students. We began talking about the possibility of doing a field trip with a group of third and fourth graders to Bosque del Apache, a bird and wildlife refuge near Socorro, New Mexico; and writing poems there for submission to River of Words (see chapter 5). But a limited budget and the constraints of the calendar soon got in the way of these plans.

So we took a leap into the unknown. I had been to Bosque, and I am fascinated by birds and their migrations. I was anxious to learn more. We planned a program with the following components:

Before the Visit

- E-mail introductions, including my perspective on rivers and natural places, and my approach to writing in a special place like Bosque.
- Teacher Sue Borchers conducted an orientation in the classroom, including reading a sample poem from the River of Words web site. Discussion included some of these topics: What do you think it looked like when the child who wrote that poem visited her river? What's it going to look like when we go to Bosque? Look at map of that section of Rio Grande. Where does Bosque fit with our river? Talk about looking at the river from far away, as in a map; from closer up, as in someone else's writing about it; and from very close. What do you see differently with each shift of focus?

  She also led a brief discussion on using senses on the field trip.
- Sue role-played the place with the children: they chose the roles of various kinds of perching birds (bluebirds, flycatchers); predatory birds (hawks, eagles); and water birds (cranes, snow geese). They picked movements (standing in place) that symbolized their birds. Each movement had to be linked to what it feels like to be the bird — small and fluttery, large and powerful, watchful, etc. Some kids played the part of the lake itself, the road winding round it, all the way back to Camino Real days, the reeds growing on the shore, the clouds floating through the sky, the sun watching.
- The class generated words from this exercise. Sue reminded the kids that when they went through the place, they'd be captur-

ing words just like this — putting them down, then using them to make poems. She introduced poetry, discussed basics of a poem: words, lines, stanzas. Sometimes rhyming, but not always.

DURING THE VISIT

The group followed general guidelines for writing in place (see chapter 3). They walked the trail, stopped, wrote, gathered impressions. I had sent material on several different structures that could be tried, so the kids had many possible "containers" for their words. They could write list poems, they could write in a bird's voice, they could repeat lines in set patterns for effect. Adults on the trip also wrote, and everybody shared work in progress at various points. I had told them in my introductory messages, "If you want to climb a fence, pull up a plant, throw a rock, jump in the lake, do anything else you know the park won't want you to do, write about it instead of using your body."

FOLLOWING THE FIELD TRIP

The class shared poem drafts with each other, and through e-mail, with me. I reviewed all the poems, and sent them back with detailed comments. The poems were startling in their clarity, and in how minutely these very young children had been able to look at the place they visited. I asked questions where intent or meaning was unclear, and let them know the ultimate decision for changes rested with them. Some children wrote back to clarify lines, ask questions, make comments. Some accepted my suggestions. Some didn't. But all were excited by the process, and all brought me to a vivid appreciation of the day they had spent, walking, and writing. It was all so exciting that even two kids who hadn't made it on the field trip ended up writing poems, interviewing classmates to "get" what they had seen.

The class went back to Bosque when the poems were complete, and read them at a reception. The only thing that didn't work about the whole process was that I kept wishing I could have been there in person! Here is one of the poems from that virtual residency:

Cattails
by Kayla Cline

Cattails live in the water
Cattails look like corn dogs,
on a long stick.

If you cannot get to a place, there are sometimes ways in which that place can get to you. Arts in the Parks is a traveling exhibition of representative art, sponsored by a privately funded agency, the National Parks Academy of the Arts (see appendix 1). Based in Jackson Hole, Wyoming, the organization runs a national campaign to solicit entries to a painting competition. The paintings judged to be the top 100 constitute a national touring exhibition, and the Academy works closely with the National Park Foundation to help publicize the parks represented in each year's exhibit. Artists' entry fees, standard practice in the juried art show world, pays for competition prize money. Participating artists receive a flat fee royalty, and a percentage of the money received from sale of paintings.

Each year, a tour schedule is set up by the National Parks Academy. The exhibition sometimes hangs in art galleries, sometimes in city art centers, sometimes in Park Service facilities. Additionally, the National Park Foundation has established an official collection of this art, from which paintings are made available on request to National Park headquarters, museums, corporations, and government facilities that might not be able to display a show as large as the Top 100, but are still interested in showcasing realistic art depicting National Park settings. (See appendix 1 for contact information.)

Sometimes space to display student work is limited. When that work is in the form of writing, an option might be to consider publication. While several in-school publication options are now available to teachers, one worth considering is online publishing, which can offer students and teachers the opportunity to enter and edit work in a web-based forum.

WordRunner Chapbooks is a start-to-finish small press service— designing, printing and binding affordable, quality booklets of 16 to 64 pages, suitable for poetry, short stories or essays, recipe collections, family histories, memoirs, or children's stories.

Chapbooks are slender booklets, half the size of a letter sized sheet of paper; the covers are stapled twice at the spine. The books are printed in editions of no more than 100 copies. Inside pages for these limited editions are high resolution laser prints, typeset from the manuscript or computer disk you submit. The WordRunner web site (see appendix 1) gives details of price, format, and style. Sample chapbooks of poetry are also available.

It is likely that as e-publishing in general grows, there will be other sites offering ways to produce collections of student work in small print runs at relatively low cost.

Several major parks and museums now offer web sites with information in varying levels of detail about exhibits, curatorial and interpretive philosophies, and outreach programs of their own. It is possible, for example, to download a virtual gallery of images from, say poet Kenneth Patchen's artfully simple-seeming picture poems, and then have students work on integrating their own writing ideas, Patchen-style, with visual images of protest against injustice and war. There is also a wealth of online resources for mathematics, the physical and natural sciences, language arts, history, geography—the content areas are evolving daily. With a little instruction, students can be taught to differentiate between junk sites and those offering credible information. For younger grades, the internet can serve as a vast repository of information that can be accessed and pulled into lesson planning by a teacher interested in departing from textbook-based instruction. Internet resources from a sampling of areas is provided in appendix 1.

Whatever the sources we might gain our understanding from—virtual or real, artistic or scientific—we humans are linked to the places we inhabit. In the introduction to *Through the Eyes of Children* (a field guide to western Colorado and the Colorado plateau), the children of Tope Elementary School wrote, "This is a region unlike any other. . . . Learn to love it as we have." Their words might hold meaning for all of us, for in a very real sense, each of the special places we choose to teach in and about is a place "like no other."

$\mathcal{A}$ppendix One

Resources

NATIONAL PARKS SERVICE EDUCATIONAL PROGRAMS

National Trust for Historic
Preservation
1785 Massachusetts Avenue NW
Washington DC 20036
202–588–6000 or 800–944–6847
http://www.nthp.org

Parks as Classrooms
National Park Service
PO Box 37127
Washington DC 20013-7127
http://www.nps.gov/interp/
parkclass.html

Teaching with Historic Places
National Register of Historic
Places

National Park Service
1849 C Street NW, Suite 400
Washington DC 20240
http://www.cr.nps.gov/nr/twhp

RELATED RESOURCES

Council for the Interpretation of
Native People
National Association for
Interpretation
P.O. Box 2246
Fort Collins CO 80522
970–484–8283
970–484–8179, fax
888–900–8283, toll-free
http://www.interpnet.com

National Endowment for the
Humanities
1100 Pennsylvania Avenue NW
Washington DC 20506
202–606-8400
e-mail: info@neh.gov
http://www.neh.fed.us/

National History Day
0119 Cecil Hall
University of Maryland
College Park MD 20742
301–314–9739
e-mail:
National.History.Day@umail.um
d.edu
http://www.thehistorynet.com/
NationalHistoryDay/

The National Parks Academy of
the Arts
PO Box 608
Jackson Hole WY 83001
800–553-2787
307–739–1199 fax
e-mail: artsfortheparks@
blissnet.com
http://www.artsfortheparks.com

National Science Resources Center
955 L'Enfant Plaza SW, Suite 8400
Washington DC 20560–0952
202–287–2063

SCHOOL- AND COMMUNITY-BASED EDUCATIONAL PROGRAMS AND RESOURCES

Diane Hirschinger Gallegos
(*Through the Eyes of the
Children*, a field guide published
by students of Tope Elementary
School, Grand Junction CO)
3324 Music Lane
Grand Junction CO 81506
970–243-1565

Muncaster Challenge Program
Attn.: Reginald Smith
6300 Muncaster Mill Road
Rockville MD 20855
301–548–4960
http://www.mcps.k12.md.us/
schools/muncaster

Park-It!
City of Toledo
Department of Parks,
Recreation, and Forestry
Attn.: Dennis Garvin
26 Main Street
Toledo OH 43605–2032
419–936-2875

River of Words
International Rivers Network
PO Box 4000–J
Berkeley CA 94704
510–433-7020
510–848–1008 fax
e-mail: row@irn.org
http://www.riverofwords.org

CURRICULUM RESOURCES

Center for Children's
Environmental Literature
Attn.: Lynne Cherry
PO Box 5995
Washington DC 20016

Judyth Hill
(Poet-in-Residence, Georgia
O'Keeffe Museum)
HC 69, Box 20H
Sapello NM 87745

Idaho Water Institute
Morrill Hall, Room 205
University of Idaho
Moscow ID 83844–3011
208–885–2170
208–885–6431 fax
e-mail: empower2@uidaho.edu

North Carolina Division of Parks
and Recreation
Attn.: Martha Kane
Lead, Interpretation and
Education
12700 Bayleaf Church Road
Raleigh NC 27614
919–846-9991
e-mail: marti.kane@ncmail.net

Storyline Design
Attn.: Jeff Creswell/Scottish
Storyline Method
PMB 246
333 State Street
Lake Oswego OR 97034
503-288–1132
e-mail: creswell@teleport.com

Sandra Pfeifer, Filmmaker
(*Kathryn and Her Daughters*)
RR# 1 Box 278
Simpson IL 62985
618–695–3544

Teachers and Writers
Collaborative
5 Union Square West
New York NY 10003-3306
888–BOOKS-TW
http://www.writenet.org

OTHER ORGANIZATIONS WITH ENVIRONMENTAL EDUCATION PROGRAMS AND MATERIALS

American Museum of Natural History
Central Park West at 79th Street
New York NY 10024–5192
212–769–5000
http://www.amnh.org

Coastal Conservation Association
4801 Woodway, Stuite 220W
Houston TX 77056
800–201–FISH
http://www.joincca.org

The Cousteau Society, Inc.
870 Greenbrier Circle, Suite 402
Chesapeake VA 23320
800–441–4395
http://www.cousteausociety.org

National Arbor Day Foundation
100 Arbor Avenue
Nebraska City NE 68410
http://www.arborday.org

National Wildlife Federation
11100 Wildlife Center Drive
Reston VA 20190
703–438–6000
http://www.nwf.org

The Nature Conservancy
4245 Fairfax Drive, Suite 100
Arlington VA 22203
800–628–6860
http://www.tnc.org

The Wilderness Society
1615 M Street NW
Washington DC 20036
1–800–THE-WILD

ONLINE RESOURCES

Please note: Internet sites and URLs change frequently, so frequent updating of your bookmarks is recommended. URLs selected here represent established organizations and individuals dedicated to their work, so even if a site has moved, a keyword search should find it again quite easily.

Aaron Shepard's RT Page
(Scripts & Tips for Reader's Theater)
http://www.aaronshep.com/rt/
Aaron Shepard is a children's writer and an old hand at Reader's Theater. The site includes tips, practice sheets, recommended script collections, and links to related sites.

Community Stewardship
Exchange
http://www.sonoran.org
*Includes information, contacts
and examples of community-
based strategies for sustainable
development.*

The Foundation Center
http://www.fdncenter.org
*Includes a Foundation Finder, and
a link to a subscription based "24/7
access" database, The Foundation
Directory Online Plus.*

The Heritage Education Network
(THEN)
http://www.mtsu.edu/~then
*Lesson plans, activities, checklists,
Visual Survey forms, bibliogra-
phies, and other teaching resources.*

Imperial War Museum (United
Kingdom)
http://www.iwm.org.uk/
lambeth/online.htm
*Online exhibitions include a range
of subjects related to the two
World Wars and the inter-war
period. Teacher packets can be
ordered, but payment must be in
pounds sterling. Oral history
interviews can be downloaded
from sound archive.*

Library of Congress
http://www.loc.gov/
Follow links to American
Memory pages, or for the
American Memory Learning
Page, go to
http://memory.loc.gov/ammem/
ndlpedu/index.html
*Houses searchable historic collec-
tions for the National Digital
Library. Each individual
American Memory collection
includes archival text and images,
and is accompanied by lesson
plans and reading lists.*

My History
http://www.myhistory.org
*A demonstration millennium
project of the National
Endowment for the Humanities.
Kids can explore a historic time-
line, exchange family stories, and
learn about family treasures as
vestiges of history.*

Oregon Public Education
Network
http://www.open.k12.or.us/start/
visual/featured/artbook/index.
html.
*This site describes book art projects
developed to meet Oregon standards. It is aimed at teachers, and
offers directions for making simple
books, plus good ideas for writing
and illustrating stories. Directions
are clear and simple and there are
good diagrams. Includes instructions for making paste papers.*

PUMAS (Practical Uses of Math
and Science)
http://pumas.jpl.nasa.gov/
*Described as the online journal of
math and science examples for
pre-college education, this site
hosts plans on topics as diverse as
hypothermia in a Laura Ingalls
Wilder book and mathematical
estimation of the global consequences of everyday actions.
Additions to the database are wel-
comed.*

Rivers & Trails/National Park
Service
http://www.ncrc.nps.gov/rtca/rtc
a-we.htm
Rivers & Trails helps carry out the

*National Park Service mission by
working with local citizen groups
to revitalize nearby rivers, pre-
serve valuable open spaces, and
develop local trail and greenway
networks. NPS offers resources
and linkages, not funding.*

Smithsonian Institution
http://www.si.edu/
*Links to Smithsonian without
Walls, a downloadable interactive
series of virtual exhibitions created
especially for Internet use. Still in
prototype stage but available for
public review and comment.*

Teaching with Historic Places
http://www.cr.nps.gov/nr/twhp/
*Online lesson plans are available
from this educational site main-
tained by the National Register of
Historic Places.*

WordRunner
http://www.wordrunner.com
*Home-office/publishing small
business in the San Francisco area
with an internet presence.
Manuscripts can be submitted
electronically and prices vary with
quantities ordered.*

*A*ppendix *T*wo

Art from the Global Scrap-Heap: Sample Material from a Museum-Developed Teacher Guide

*T*his teacher guide was developed for use with an exhibition of folk art underscoring the aesthetics of recycled objects. Curriculum connections are clear from these excerpted examples, and can be easily replicated, using a museum exhibition near you, and connecting a visit to it with your state performance standards.

RECYCLED, RE-SEEN: FOLK ART FROM THE GLOBAL SCRAP-HEAP

HOW THIS EXHIBITION CAN FIT INTO THE CALIFORNIA VISUAL AND PERFORMING ARTS FRAMEWORK

Example 1: Artistic Perception Component

> **Goal 1.** Students use their senses to perceive works of art, objects in nature, events, and their environment.

> Pre-visit activity: Using the color images provided, ask students what they perceive an object might be made of (what is the material?). Have students discuss where the artist might have found the material. How could the material have been used differently?

Is there another reusable material that might work better? Why or why not?

Post-visit activity: Using your choice of available media, ask the students to remember their favorite object from the exhibition. There are over 800 objects in the exhibition. Ask them to focus on one. Have them discuss their observations about the object. Discuss the materials, the texture, the size, the shape, and any other physical properties of the object. Assign the students to draw their object, paying close attention to the physical properties they just discussed.

Example 2: Artistic Perception Component

Goal 2. Students identify visual structures and functions of art, using the language of the visual arts.

Pre-visit activity: Select an image from the color images provided. Ask the students, "Can you find line in this work?" How does the artist use line? Are the lines straight?

Post-visit activity: Have students think of an object in the exhibition that used many lines. How are lines important to this object? Do they have a function? Why or why not?

Example 3: Historic and Cultural Context Component

Goal 3. Students explore the role of the visual arts in culture and human history.

Pre-visit activity: Select a color image. Ask students what country the object is from. Could it have been made hundreds of years ago? (The discarded materials are very modern). Why might the artist have made the item? Is it important to a ceremony? Is it utilitarian?

Post-visit activity: There are 800 objects from over fifty-two countries. What were the differences and similarities that could be seen?

This exhibition and the associated teacher packet also offered an array of facts about recycling—steps taken locally and regionally, and the negative facts about accumulating garbage and consumer waste. Curriculum links suggest activities such as writing letters to toy, food, or mail order companies about their packaging practices; developing a practical way to separate recyclable articles using a fan, water, and a magnet; and comparison-shopping by breaking down the cost of bulk packaging versus individual packaging, comparing price to weight/volume, etc.

Appendix Three

Georgia O'Keeffe Museum Poetry Curriculum

Judyth Hill of Sapello, New Mexico, urges people everywhere to "Put a Spin on the Planet: Write a Poem." The Georgia O'Keeffe Museum in Santa Fe, New Mexico is the only museum dedicated solely to the life and work of a female artist. It features works by O'Keeffe in a variety of mediums from all periods of her life, as well as traveling exhibits of work by artists who influenced her or were influenced by her. The museum has developed a comprehensive outreach program, to forge links with educators and community groups both in the area and elsewhere, including include a nationally recognized art and leadership program for girls. In the museum itself, exhibitions are often enhanced by quotes from O'Keeffe in wall text. An introductory video provides background information on her life and art. O'Keeffe broke with the landscape art traditions of her time in creating huge, vibrant images of objects such as flowers and bleached bones in the desert, setting them against earth and sky in unconventional ways. Her art therefore offers students visual prompts for using language in similarly bold and beautiful ways.

Here is an excerpt from the poetry curriculum (associated with an exhibition bearing the same name) that Judyth Hill, poetry diva, developed for the Georgia O'Keeffe Museum. The activities are meant to be carried out in conjunction with a visit to the museum, although they could also work in a "classroom gallery" that would include posters from the museum.

POETRY OF THINGS

Apple Exercise

This works with very small children, with parents acting as scribes, as well as with older children and adults.

All participants are given a fresh apple, paper, and pencils.

We begin by making exact visual observations of the apple, looking with clarity and concentration, taking note of the details of the apple.

Next, we experience the apple with the other senses: listening to our apples (with many fun discoveries such as the lovely hollow sound when tapped!); smelling; feeling; and finally tasting. It is important to make observations of each sensory category aloud. Sharing adds to the vividness of the cumulative experience, and also helps the group to coalesce.

With very young children, it is possible to do this part of the exercise orally. With older children and adults, it is good to have participants begin by taking loose notes of observations, including those of the art, the place in which it is housed, and others in the group.

Then, using a clay that can be taken home and baked to harden, all the participants sculpt an apple, using their grounded experience of the apples to make an "art" apple.

Next, invite the students to close their eyes, positioning their hands as if they held an invisible apple.

Then, lead the group through a guided imagery experience, recreating the appearance, smell, taste, sound, and heft of the apple, this time including a memory experience (apples they have held, smelled, tasted before!). Then, have them open their eyes, come back into the room, and realize that they had a very vibrant and intimate experience of the purely imaginary!

With that under their belts, participants are ready to make another translation from imagination into artistic expression: writing about apples.

All the writing is shared aloud.

Thus prepared, enter the museum, and spend some time looking at O'Keeffe's views of apples.

This exercise works with two important concepts in the exhibition—the power of the imagination, and finding art in the everyday. The first has to do with a literal understanding of "poem," from the Greek word, *poiema*, which means something made or created, and the understanding that poetry's most distinguishing feature is its imaginative power. The apple work allows students to experience aspects of O'Keeffe's artistic expression, using the tools of writing.

Simple Presence Poems

Once inside, make sure students have paper and pencil. Select a room. Students are asked to look carefully at the paintings, and then decide which one they just love.

They then sit on the floor directly in front of their painting. A simple formula is explained, and line by line, they write a poem on site. Then students share their work, reading aloud.

One formula is:

> I see . . .
> I hear . . .
> I taste . . .
> I smell . . .
> I feel . . .
> I remember . . .

To this can be added, I dream. . . , I believe. . . , I wish. . . , I love. . . , I know. . .

These can be re-ordered, to enhance the lesson, and to add a component of composition to the experience.

The exercise can also be introduced with the instruction to find a painting that mystifies or even bothers the viewer; then the act of relating to the painting with poetry is suffused with exploration, and possibly, enlightenment.

Another formula that can be used, completing each line with an object from a painting, is:

> I seem to be . . .
> But really I'm . . .

Or,

> I used to be . . .
> But now I'm . . .

1. Use the above phrases as beginnings of lines that alternate and repeat. Students can start with an image of their own in the first line, and then complete the second line with an image from a particular painting.

Example:

> I seem to be a piece of string,
> But really I'm a ladder.

2. The exercise can then be repeated, reversing this pattern. Students can use an image from the painting in the first line, then an image of their own in the next.

3. For really interesting results, you can open the exercise to include all the paintings in a single room, so that students need not be limited to a single piece of art in their writing. Then the poems capture both the diversity of the paintings, and the cohesiveness of a themed gallery exhibition.

Synesthesia

This is an exercise in untying our usual associations. Its relevance to the *Poetry of Things* exhibit lies in the fact that Georgia O'Keeffe would often listen to violin music, stargaze, and draw associatively, to explore what might come of such experiences.

Before entering the museum, students listen to music, and to poetry read out loud. They also draw with colored pencils, or paint loose, relaxing paintings with watercolors.

Then students are asked to quiet down. They enter the show silently, find a painting, sit, and write for ten to twenty minutes.

This writing should be shared aloud, the process discussed, and individual experiences compared.

Composition Exercise

This exercise focuses on structure and placement as a primary element in making art. Conceptually, this is an important key to understanding O'Keeffe's approach to painting.

Entering the museum with paper and pen, the students should be invited to stroll about making relaxed notes on all they observe, overhear, smell, feel, remember, fantasize about, and so on. They should be encouraged to include many images and colors from the paintings, but also to include titles, snippets from the O'Keeffe quotes on the walls, lines from the video. The process leads them to become receptive, gently selective instruments.

The important detail here is that all these observations, perceptions, and quotes should be jotted down, as much as possible, in the form of single lines as for poems.

Then students should return to a workshop space, where three or four copies of their work can be photocopied. Students will then cut out the separate lines of their writing with scissors.

Now the fun part! On beautiful paper of varying colors and weights, the lines should be arranged, and then rearranged, and several poems made by each student. Poems can then be shared.

Again, it is very important that participants discuss what happened for them in the composing and arranging processes.

Moving from Natural to Abstract Forms

This exercise plays off the preceding one.

A group enters the museum with paper, pencils, and the instruction to select challenging and intriguing images and colors from the paintings. View the entire show, making this list.

This list will then include simple, real items: white pelvis bone, black hollyhock, adobe wall in sunlight, cobalt blue sky, apples.

Then the group should go to a workshop room and begin the process of fitting these images of natural objects together in such a way that they create a narrative of juxtaposition and contrast, that will probably be quite surreal.

> Apples lie in a pool of sky,
> white bone floats above the door.
> Everything is speaking adobe –
> Hollyhocks listen, transfixed.

This writing will be a stretch, but again, the writer's various struggles and triumphs should be discussed.

Pantoum

This is a fifteenth century Malayan form that adapts excellently to working with visual art, and by its very nature, makes for lyrical, evocative poetry.

Enter the museum with paper and pencil. Slowly tour one of the rooms, so that the mood is quiet and ruminative.

Then, have the group sit. Calmly, gently, students will write a four line stanza (quatrain) that will begin their poem. Stress that it is a beginning.

Tell them then, to write the second quatrain, using this pattern:

Lines 2 and 4 of the preceding stanza are repeated as lines 1 and 3 of the next stanza. For example:

> There is something we never say about bones,
> and secrets held in folds of lily.
> Somewhere, surely, plates of ripe fruit balance on gray sills,
> while skyscrapers rise beyond those footed bowls.

And secrets held in folds of lily,
open out, reveal a bright expanse of blue,
while skyscrapers rise beyond those footed bowls,
as if foreground was the real mystery.

Then go on, perhaps three to five stanzas. When students are ready to write their closing stanzas, tell them that the second and forth lines of the last stanza should be the same lines as the third and first lines of the opening stanza. Thus, every line is used twice, and the first line and last line are the same.

Open out, reveal a bright expanse of blue
Somewhere, surely, plates of ripe fruit balance on gray sills.
As if foreground was the real mystery,
There is something we never say about bones,

This exercise could also be used as means of focusing on the theme of repetition as an element in O'Keeffe's work.

Other activities in the Poetry of Things curriculum include creating a sestina; an exercise on opposition, transition, repetition, and symmetry that includes material on O'Keeffe's relationship to the ideas of her teacher, Arthur Wesley Dow; story writing prompted by a painting; and writing poems to painting titles. Using this curriculum as a model, teachers can develop their own ways of using art in museum settings as a stimulus to their own writing and that of their students.

$\mathcal{A}$PPENDIX $\mathcal{F}$OUR

State Arts Councils

Alabama State Council on the
Arts
201 Monroe Street
Montgomery AL 36130–1800
334–242–4076

Alaska State Council on the Arts
411 West 4th Avenue, Suite 1E
Anchorage AK 99501–2343
907–269–6610
email:asca@alaska.net

American Samoa Council on
Culture, Arts and Humanities
PO Box 1540
Office of the Governor
Pago Pago AS 96799
684-633-4347

Arizona Commission on the Arts
417 West Roosevelt Street
Phoenix AZ 85003
602–255–5882

Arkansas Arts Council
1500 Tower Building
323 Center Street
Little Rock AR 72201
email: info@dah.state.ar.us

California Arts Council
1300 I Street, Suite 930
Sacramento CA 95814
916-322–6555
email: cac@cwo.com

Colorado Council on the Arts
750 Pennsylvania Street
Denver CO 80203-3699
303-894–2617
email: coloarts@ix.netcom.com

Connecticut Commission on
the Arts
One Financial Plaza
755 Main Street
Hartford CT 06103
850–566-4770

Delaware Division of the Arts
Carvel State Office Building
820 North French Street, 4th
floor
Wilmington DE 19801
302–577–8278
email: delarts@artswire.org

District of Columbia (DC)
Commission on the Arts and
Humanities
410 8th Street NW, 5th floor
Washington DC 20004
202–724–5613
email: dccah@erols.com

Florida Division of Cultural
Affairs
The Capitol
Tallahassee FL 32399–0250
850–487–2980

Georgia Council for the Arts
260 14th Street NW, Suite 401
Atlanta GA 30318
404–685–ARTS (2787)

Guam Council on the Arts and
Humanities Agency
PO Box 2950
Agana GU 96910
671–475–CAHA (2242/3)

Hawaii State Foundation on
Culture and the Arts
44 Merchant Street
Honolulu HI 96813
808–586-0300
email: sfca@sfca.state.hi.us

Idaho Commission on the Arts
304 West State Street
Boise ID 83702–0008
208–334–6750

Illinois Arts Council
100 West Randolph Street
Suite 10–500
Chicago IL 60601

Indiana Arts Commission
402 W Washington Street
Room W072
Indianapolis IN 46204
317–232–1268

Iowa Arts Council
Capitol Complex
600 E Locust
Des Moines IA 50319
515–281–4451

Kansas Arts Commission
Jayhawk Tower
700 SW Jackson, Suite 1004
Topeka KS 66603-3761
785–296-3335

Kentucky Arts Council
Old Capitol Annex
300 W Broadway
Frankfort KY 40601
502–564–3757

Louisiana Division of the Arts
PO Box 44247
Baton Rouge LA 70804
225–342–8180

Maine Arts Commission
55 Capitol Street
State House Station 25
Augusta ME 04333
207–287–2724

Maryland State Arts Council
601 North Howard Street,
1st floor
Baltimore MD 21201
410–767–6555

Massachusetts Cultural Council
120 Boylston Street, 2nd floor
Boston MA 02116-4600
617–727–3668

Michigan Council for the Arts
and Cultural Affairs
G. Mennan Williams Bldg.,
3rd floor
525 West Ottawa/POB 30705
Lansing MI 48909–8205
517–241–4011

Minnesota State Arts Board
Park Square Court
400 Sibley Street, Suite 200
St. Paul MN 55102
651–215–1600

Mississippi Arts Commission
239 North Lamar Street,
2nd floor
Jackson MS 39201
601–359–6030 or 6040

Missouri Arts Council
111 North 7th Street, Suite 105
St. Louis MO 63101
314–340–6845

Montana Arts Council
City Council Building
316 North Park Avenue,
Suite 252
Helena MT 59620–2201
406-444–6430
email: mac@state.mt.us

Nebraska Arts Council
3838 Davenport
Omaha NE 68131–2329
402–595–2122

Nevada Arts Council
602 North Curry Street
Carson City NV 89703
775–687–6680

New Hampshire State Council
on the Arts
40 North Main Street,
Phenix Hall
Concord NH 03301–4974
603-271–2789

New Jersey State Council on the
Arts
225 West State Street
POB 306
Trenton NJ 08625
609–292–6130

New Mexico Arts
228 East Palace Avenue
Santa Fe NM 87501
505–827–6490

New York State Council on the
Arts
915 Broadway, 8th floor
New York NY 10010
212–387–7000

North Carolina Arts Council
Department of Cultural
Resources
Raleigh NC 27699–4632
919–733-2821 ext 20

North Dakota Council on the Arts
418 East Broadway, Suite 70
Bismarck ND 58501–4086
701–328–3956

Commonwealth Council for Arts
and Culture
(Northern Mariana Islands)
PO Box 5553, CHRB
Saipan MP 96950
011–670–322–9982 or 9983
email: galaidi@gtepacifica.net

Ohio Arts Council
727 East Main Street
Columbus OH 43205
614–466-2613

Oklahoma Arts Council
Jim Thorpe Building
PO Box 52001–2001
Oklahoma City OK 73152–2001
405–521–2931

Oregon Arts Commission
775 Summer Street NE
Salem OR 97310
503-986-0088

Pennsylvania Council on the Arts
216 Finance Building
Harrisburg PA 17120
717–787–6883 ext 3028

Institute of Puerto Rican Culture
PO Box 9024184
San Juan PR 00902–4184
787–725–5137

Rhode Island State Council on
the Arts
95 Cedar Street, Suite 103
Providence RI 02903-1034
401–222–3880

South Carolina Arts Commission
1800 Gervais Street
Columbia SC 29201
803-734–8696

South Dakota Arts Council
Office of the Arts
800 Governors Drive
Pierre SD 57501–2294
605–773-3131

Tennessee Arts Commission
Citizens Plaza
401 Charlotte Avenue
Nashville TN 37243-0780
615–741–1701

Texas Commission on the Arts
PO Box 13406, Capitol Station
Austin TX 78711
512–463-5535
front.desk@arts.state.tx.us

Utah Arts Council
613 East South Temple Street
Salt Lake City UT 84102
801–236-7555

Vermont Arts Council
136 State Street, Drawer 33
Montpelier VT 05633-6001
802–828–3291
email: info@arts.vca.state.vt.us

Virgin Islands Council on the
Arts
41–42 Norregade
PO Box 103
St. Thomas VI 00804
340–774–5984
email: vicouncil@islands.vi

Virginia Commission for the
Arts
223 Governor Street, 2nd floor
Richmond VA 23219
804–225–3132
email: vacomm@artswire.org

Washington State Arts
Commission
234 East 8th Avenue
PO Box 42675
Olympia WA 98504–2673
360–586-2423

West Virginia Commission on
the Arts
1900 Kanawha Blvd East
Charleston WV 25305
304–558–0240

Wisconsin Arts Board
101 East Wilson Street,
1st floor
Madison WI 53702
608–266-0190
email: rtertin@arts.state.wi.us

Wyoming Arts Council
2320 Capitol Avenue
Cheyenne WY 82002
307–777–7742
email: wyoarts@artswire.org

Appendix Five

Private Nonprofit Organizations with Programs on Public Land

Appalachian Mountain Club
Claudia Thompson
5 Joy Street
Boston MA 02108
617–523-0636
http://www.outdoors.org

Canyonlands Field Institute
Karla Vander Zanden
PO Box 68
Moab UT 84532
801–259–7750
http://canyonlandsfieldinst.org

Crow Canyon Archeological
Center
Bruce Grimes
23390 County Road K
Cortez CO 81321
970–565–8975
http://crowcanyan.org

Denali Foundation
Willy Karidis
PO Box 212
Denali AK 99755
907–683-2597
http://denali.org

Four Corners School of Outdoor
Education
Janet Ross
PO Box 1029
Monticello UT 84532
801–587–2156
http://www.fourcornersschool.
org

Glacier Institute
Kris Bruninga
PO Box 7457
Kalispell MT 59904
406-755–1211
http://glacierinstitute.org

Grand Canyon Field Institute
Mike Buchheit
PO Box 399
Grand Canyon AZ 86023
520–638–2485
http://www.grandcanyon.org/
fieldinstitute

Great Smoky Mountains
Institute
Ken Voorhis
9275 Tremont Road
Townsend TN 37882
423-448–6709
http://www.nps.gov/grsm/
tremont.htm

Headlands Institute
(Yosemite National Institutes)
Bruce Truitt
Building 1033
Golden Gate National Recreation
Area
Sausalito CA 94965
415–332–5771
http://www.yni.org

Keystone Science School
Chris Chopyak-Minor
PO Box 8606
Keystone CO 80435
303-468–5824
http://www.keystone.org

Olympic Park Institute
(Yosemite National Institutes)
Maitland Peet
111 Barnes Point Road
Port Angeles WA 98363
360–928–3720

Oregon Museum of Science &
Industry
Joe Jones
7171 S.W. Quarry Drive
Redmond OR 97756
541–548–5473
http://www.omsi.edu

Pocono Environmental
Education Center
Jack Padalino
RR #2, Box 1010
Dingman's Ferry PA 18328
570–828–8200
http://www.peec.org

Rocky Mountain National
Association
Nancy Wilson
Rocky Mountain National Park
Estes Park CO 80517
970–586–0108

Teton Science School
Jack Shea
PO Box 68
Kelly WY 83011
307–733-4765
http://www.tetonscience.org

Yellowstone Institute
Jeff Brown
PO Box 117
Yellowstone WY 82190
307–344–2295
http://www.yellowstone.net

Yosemite Institute
(Yosemite National Institutes)
Michael Lee
PO Box 487
Yosemite CA 95389
209–379–9511
http://www.yni.org

ℬIBLIOGRAPHY

Arany, Lynne, and Archie Hobson. *Little Museums*. New York: Henry Holt, 1998.

Ashworth, Tammy. *Recycled, Re-Seen: Folk Art from the Global Scrap-Heap* (Teacher Packet). Palm Springs, CA: Palms Springs Desert Museum, 1998.

Blandy, Doug, and David Cowan, "iMAGiNE! Yellowstone: Art Education and the Reinhabitation of Place," *Art Education*, 50, no. 6 (November 1997): 40-46.

Bruchac, Joseph. "The Continuing Circle: Native American Storytelling Past and Present." In *Who Says? Essays on Pivotal Issues in Contemporary Storytelling* edited by Carol Birch and Melissa Heckler. Little Rock, AR: August House, 1996.

Cowan, David. Personal communication, December 1999.

Creswell, Jeff. *Creating Worlds, Constructing Meaning*. Portsmouth, NH: Heinemann, 1997.

Dubin, Steven C. *Displays of Power: Memory and Amnesia in the American Museum.* New York: New York University Press, 1999.

DuFour, Marilyn. Personal communication, December 1999.

Galt, Margot Fortunato. *The Story in History: Writing Your Way into the American Experience.* New York: Teachers & Writers Collaborative, 1992.

Garvin, Dennis. Personal communication, December 1999.

George, Kristine O'Connell. *Old Elm Speaks: Tree Poems.* New York: Clarion Books, 1999.

Hakim, Joy. *The First Americans.* Book 1, *A History of Us.* New York: Oxford University Press, 1993.

Hakim, Joy. Personal communication, February 2000.

Ham, Sam H. *Environmental Interpretation: A Practical Guide for People with Big Ideas and Small Budgets.* Golden, CO: North American Press, 1992.

Harvey, Stephanie. *Nonfiction Matters.* York, ME: Stenhouse Publishers, 1998.

Hollis, Cynthia, "On Developing an Art and Ecology Curriculum," *Art Education*, 50, no. 6 (November 1997): 21-24.

Huyck, Heather, "Beyond John Wayne: Using Historic Sites to Interpret Western Women's History," *OAH Magazine of History* (Fall 1997): 7-11.

Johnson, Paul. *A Book of One's Own.* New York: Heinemann, 1998.

King, Casey, and Linda Barrett Osborne. *Oh, Freedom.* New York: Alfred A. Knopf, 1997.

Komissar, Cheska, Debra Hart, Robin Friedlander, Susan Tufts, and
Maria Paiewonsky. *Don't Forget the Fun: Developing Inclusive
Recreation.* Boston: Institute for Community Inclusion, Boston
Children's Hospital, 1997.

Moon, M. Sherril, editor. *Making School and Community Recreation
Fun for Everyone.* Baltimore: Paul H. Brookes, 1994.

Pfeifer, Sandra, producer. *Kathryn and Her Daughters.* Videotape.
Simpson, IL: 2000.

Project Rec. *Making It Accessible: Accommodation Strategies.* Boston:
Children's Hospital, 1993.

Schleien, Stuart J., Leo H. McAvoy, Gregory J. Lais, and John E.
Rynders. *Integrated Outdoor Education and Adventure Programs.*
Champaign, IL: Sagamore Publishing, 1993.

Super, Paul, "Cool Wings," *Walker Valley Reflections,* Winter 1999-
2000:9.

Tilden, Freeman. *Interpreting Our Heritage.* Chapel Hill, NC:
University of North Carolina Press, 1957.

Winks, Robin. In *Parks As Classrooms.* Videotape. Harpers Ferry, WV:
National Park Service Division of Audiovisual Arts, 1992.

INDEX